Systematic Theology Workbook

Systematic Theology Workbook

Wayne Grudem
Brianna Smith
and Erik Thoennes

ivp

INTER-VARSITY PRESS
36 Causton Street, London SW1P 4ST, England
Email: ivp@ivpbooks.com
Website: www.ivpbooks.com

This book is published jointly with Zondervan Academic, 3900 Sparks Dr. SE, Grand Rapids, Michigan 49546, USA

First published 2020

British Library Cataloguing-in-Publication Data
A catalogue record for this book is available from the British Library.

UK ISBN: 978–1–78974–261–9

US ISBNs: 978–0–310–11407–9 (paperback)
                  978–0–310–114086 (eBook)

Set in Garamond Premier Pro
Typeset in the United States of America
Printed and bound in Great Britain by TJ Books Ltd

Produced on paper from sustainable forests

Inter-Varsity Press publishes Christian books that are true to the Bible and that communicate the gospel, develop discipleship and strengthen the church for its mission in the world.

IVP originated within the Inter-Varsity Fellowship, now the Universities and Colleges Christian Fellowship, a student movement connecting Christian Unions in universities and colleges throughout Great Britain, and a member movement of the International Fellowship of Evangelical Students. Website: www.uccf.org.uk. That historic association is maintained, and all senior IVP staff and committee members subscribe to the UCCF Basis of Faith.

Contents

PART 4: The Doctrines of Christ and the Holy Spirit

PART 5: The Doctrine of the Application of Redemption

PART 6: The Doctrine of the Church

PART 7: The Doctrine of the Future

A Note to the Reader

For many years Wayne Grudem's *Systematic Theology* has been the primary textbook for undergraduate theology courses at Biola University where Erik has taught for twenty-one years and where Brianna has been an undergraduate and graduate student, as well as a teaching and research assistant for most of her time there. We have seen this textbook consistently help students develop greater theological depth and discernment. It was therefore a delight for us to create this workbook to help students dive more effectively into this excellent resource. The questions are intended to clarify the main points of each chapter, encourage intellectual and spiritual growth, and facilitate meaningful discussion. We hope this workbook will be used in colleges, churches, and small groups of all kinds to take students' to higher levels of understanding as well as greater academic success. Our greatest intent for this workbook, however, is the same as that of the text for which it is a companion, that knowledge of the Father, Son, and Holy Spirit will increase so that God receives greater honor and worship.

With gratitude,
Erik Thoennes and Brianna Smith

CHAPTER 1

Introduction to Systematic Theology

OPENING PRAYER

Lord, open my heart and my mind that I may discern what is true. Thank you that you are a God of order and clarity and reason, and that your Word and your ways make sense and lead to life. Teach me from the study of your Word, and allow your Spirit to transform my life through this study for your glory and honor. Amen.

CHAPTER REVIEW

1. What is systematic theology? Restate the definition in *Systematic Theology* in your own words.

2. How would Grudem define the hierarchy of authority when it comes to church history, philosophy, and Scripture?

3. What is the nature and task of systematic theology as compared and contrasted with biblical theology?

4. What is the difference between systematic theology and disorganized theology?

5. How is *doctrine* defined in this text? Restate the definition in your own words.

6. Fill in the blanks: The emphasis of systematic theology is on what God wants us to _____ and _____, while the emphasis in Christian ethics is on what God wants us to _____ and what _____ he wants us to have.

7. What is Christian ethics? Restate the definition in your own words.

8. What are the primary reasons Christians should study theology?

9. How would you describe the difference between major and minor doctrines? Give some examples of each.

10. What is the role of human reason in the study of Scripture? How does Scripture correct a wrong use of reason in any given case?

11. What is the distinction between a paradox and a contradiction?

12. What are the three steps of studying systematic theology?

    a.

    b.

    c.

THINKING CRITICALLY

13. What underlying assumptions must be made to believe that we can see and understand the whole Bible's teaching on one topic?

14. What are some objections to Grudem's method that he mentions in this chapter? Do you agree with his conclusions regarding those objections? Why or why not?

PERSONAL ENGAGEMENT

15. Having learned about the task of systematic theology, how could you put it into practice in your life?

16. What has been the foundation for your own personal beliefs? Has it been church tradition, teaching, your gut instincts, your family tradition, the Bible, or a combination of those?

17. Now that you are embarking on a study of theology through this book, what do you see as the primary value of this study in your life?

18. As you have read about the nature and task of systematic theology, what are you hoping a study of this book leads to? What are some topics that you are curious to study more?

19. What does Grudem say that "systematic theology rightly studied" leads to? Ask God for his help to allow your heart to be shaped in this way through your study.

20. As you close your time in this chapter, spend some time in prayer and worship, thanking God for the gifts he has given.

PART 1

The Doctrine of the Word of God

CHAPTER 2

The Word of God

OPENING PRAYER

Lord, "open my eyes, that I may behold wondrous things out of your law" (Ps. 119:18). You have spoken, and your Word is a light to our path and food for our souls. Give me a hunger to know you through your Word and to make you known in the proclamation of it. Amen.

CHAPTER REVIEW

1. What two things are referred to as the "Word of God"? Describe each briefly in your own words.

    a.

    b.

2. As Grudem considers speech by God, he mentions several things that the words of God do. Name some of these outcomes of God's speech.

3. What is the value of the written Word of God, the Bible? Why did Grudem choose to make the written Word the focus of his study?

THINKING CRITICALLY

4. Why do you think John refers to Jesus as the Word of God? How does learning about God's speech in the Old and New Testaments help inform your answer?

PERSONAL ENGAGEMENT

5. Do your life and habits reflect a belief that the Bible really is God's Word? How does seeing the Bible as God's very Word encourage or exhort you to engage with it?

6. As you close your time in this chapter, spend some time in prayer and worship, thanking God for his Word in flesh, Jesus; his word in speech; and his Word in text, the Bible.

CHAPTER 3

The Canon of Scripture

OPENING PRAYER

Lord, thank you that you guided your church to recognize what is inspired Holy Scripture and what is not. Help me to see how your Word reveals the Word made flesh so that we therefore need no further inspired Scripture. Help me know your Word as my very life (Deut. 32:47) and teach me how to think well about it. Amen.

CHAPTER REVIEW

1. Define *the canon of Scripture*.

2. Place the following "canon" events or authors in order chronologically: Jeremiah, Deuteronomy, the Book of the Kings of Israel, Joshua, the Ten Commandments, and Samuel.

    1.

    2.

    3.

    4.

    5.

    6.

3. What is meant by the term *Apocrypha*?

4. Why does Josephus not consider the Apocrypha "worthy of equal credit" with the books of the Old Testament?

5. Which twelve books were combined into one in the Hebrew scriptures?

6. When did the Roman Catholic Church adopt the apocryphal texts into their canon?

7. What four reasons does Grudem give for not regarding the Apocrypha as Scripture?

   1.

   2.

   3.

   4.

8. What office did many of those who wrote the New Testament hold?

9. How did the New Testament authors understand the term *Scriptures* when they used it?

10. Was all that was written by the apostles considered Scripture? Why or why not?

11. What is the ultimate reason books are considered canonical?

THINKING CRITICALLY

12. How have you seen doubt in God's Word expressed in ministry? How have you seen faith in God's Word expressed in ministry?

13. In light of what you have learned about canon, how should Christians approach Christian nonfiction books today?

14. If someone came to you claiming to have written a new book of the Bible, how would you respond to them based on what you have learned in this chapter?

PERSONAL ENGAGEMENT

15. Have you ever had someone question you regarding the legitimacy of the books of the Bible? Did you feel like you had answers to their questions? How has this chapter helped your understanding of the formation of Scripture?

16. Close your time in this chapter in prayer, thanking God for his faithfulness to preserve his Word unto this day.

CHAPTER 4

The Four Characteristics of Scripture: (1) Authority

OPENING PRAYER

Lord, teach me to submit to your Word as my authority because it comes from you (Ps 119:4). Your Word brings comfort but also conviction; it brings peace but also exposes our foolishness and sin. You are good, and all you command is good and life giving. Please give me a reverence for your Word so that the knowledge I gain will lead to my obedience to it. Amen.

CHAPTER REVIEW

1. What does Grudem state as the four characteristics (or attributes) of Scripture?

1.

2.

3.

4.

2. Define the *authority of Scripture*:

3. What does the Bible claim when it uses phrases like "Thus says the LORD"?

4. How, according to Grudem, are we convinced of the Bible's claims to be God's words?

5. What distinction does Grudem make between the Holy Spirit's evidence for the legitimacy of Scripture and other claims for the legitimacy of Scripture as God's words?

6. True / False: God dictated every word of the Bible to the human authors.

7. According to the Bible, which of the following processes did God *not* use to inspire the human authors of Scripture? (Circle your answer.)

dictation   *writing in the sand*   *historical research*   *dreams*   *visions*

8. What is the difference between saying God's words are true and that God's Word is truth?

THINKING CRITICALLY

9. How does Grudem respond to the circular argument objection? What might you add to the case against that objection?

10. What should the relationship be between Scripture and scientific fact? How does Grudem describe their relationship?

11. What role should biblical backgrounds play in interpreting Scripture?

12. Pick two doctrinal views of liberalism from the "Christianity and Theological Liberalism" appendix chart, and briefly respond to them using relevant passages.

PERSONAL ENGAGEMENT

13. When you hear "to disbelieve or disobey any word of Scripture is to disbelieve or disobey God," how does your heart respond? Are you inclined to believe Scripture? Why or why not?

14. How do you respond to the preaching of God's Word? Do you find yourself submitting to it?

15. Close your time in this chapter in prayer, thanking God for his Word, which is truth, and asking him to help you learn to treasure and submit to it rightly.

CHAPTER 5

The Inerrancy of Scripture

OPENING PRAYER

Dear Lord, help me to know that "every word of God proves true" (Prov. 30:5). You are perfect, so of course your words are perfect also. Thank you that we can be sure that your speech contains no deception or inaccuracy of any kind. You know everything and are faithful and true. Thank you that your Word reflects your character in those ways. Amen.

CHAPTER REVIEW

1. Before you read the chapter, how did you define *inerrancy*?

2. Explain the difference between saying the Bible always tells the truth and saying that it tells us every fact precisely.

3. What is the difference between infallibility and inerrancy?

4. Define *original manuscript*:

5. Why can we have confidence in the original manuscripts even though we do not have copies of them?

6. Describe textual variants in a way that a layperson in the church could understand:

7. Now, at the end of the chapter, how would you define *inerrancy*?

THINKING CRITICALLY

8. What do you think is the strongest argument for inerrancy? Restate it in your own words.

9. Do you agree with Grudem's list of problems with denying inerrancy? What would you add or take away?

PERSONAL ENGAGEMENT

10. How does confidence in the inerrancy of the Bible help you engage the text of the Bible devotionally?

11. As you finish this chapter, thank God for the truthfulness and trustworthiness of his Word.

CHAPTER 6

The Four Characteristics of Scripture: (2) Clarity

OPENING PRAYER

Lord, your Word is clear because you love to lead your children into understanding and not confusion—peace and not discord. Thank you that your Word reflects your character in this way. Please "give me understanding, that I may keep your law and observe it with my whole heart" (Ps. 119:34). Amen.

CHAPTER REVIEW

1. Rewrite the definition of *clarity of Scripture* in your own words:

2. Who is expected to be able to understand the Scriptures? (Circle all that apply.)

Pastors   *ordinary believers*   *scholars*   *adults*   *children*

3. What is the relationship between the clarity of Scripture and God holding us morally accountable for obeying his Word?

4. Complete the following chart of the requirements for understanding Scripture rightly:

Requirement	Definition (in your own words)	Scriptural Evidence
Time		
Effort		
Use of ordinary means		
Willingness to obey		
Help of the Holy Spirit		
Humble recognition that our understanding is imperfect		

5. Define the following terms:

Hermeneutics:

Exegesis:

6. How does Grudem describe the role of historical background information in understanding any given passage of Scripture?

THINKING CRITICALLY

7. Pick one of the objections to the clarity of Scripture and write your own response to it with evidence from Scripture.

8. How can we rightly talk of the complexity of interpretation of Scripture without neglecting to acknowledge its clarity?

PERSONAL ENGAGEMENT

9. Do you approach the Bible as if it is able to be understood? How do you deal with passages that are difficult to understand?

10. Using Grudem's six requirements for understanding Scripture rightly as a guide, assess your own approach when the Bible seems difficult to understand:

1. Time: Do I carve out time in my life to understand Scripture? How does my time in the Word compare with my time spent on the internet or engaging with media?

2. Effort: Do I expect understanding the Bible to be easy? What is my emotional response to the challenge of understanding God's Word?

3. The use of ordinary means: If I encounter difficulty in understanding the Bible, do I turn to other resources to help? Do I know how to access such resources? When the Word is preached to me, how do I respond? Do I see preaching as a tool to help me understand?

4. A willingness to obey: When confronted with areas of my life that are challenged by the teaching of Scripture, how do I respond?

5. The help of the Holy Spirit: Do I approach God's Word prayerfully, asking for the Spirit's help to understand, or do I do it in my own strength?

6. A humble recognition that our understanding is imperfect: Is my response to a lack of understanding in the Bible frustration or trust? Do I acknowledge my sin in my approach to Scripture?

11. End your time in this chapter by asking God to help you trust the clarity of Scripture as you engage with it in your daily life.

CHAPTER 7

The Four Characteristics of Scripture: (3) Necessity

OPENING PRAYER

Lord, without your Word we would be helpless in our quest to know you and your ways. We need to have our senses of discernment honed to discern good from evil and to know and be trained in the way of righteousness (Heb. 5:13–14). We need your Word to know that you love us and sent your Son to take away our sin. Teach me that it is by your Word that I have faith (Rom. 10:17) and life (Matt. 4:4). Amen.

CHAPTER REVIEW

1. How is the Bible necessary for salvation?

2. Why is the Bible necessary for certain knowledge about anything?

3. How can unbelievers have knowledge about God?

4. Define the following terms:

General revelation:

Special revelation:

THINKING CRITICALLY

5. Explain how Old Testament believers were saved by faith.

PERSONAL ENGAGEMENT

6. How does thinking about the necessity of Scripture help you think about evangelism and missions?

7. What do you think God is calling you to do to make his Word known to others?

8. As you finish this chapter, thank God for revealing his Word to you, and ask him to help you share it with others.

CHAPTER 8

The Four Characteristics of Scripture: (4) Sufficiency

OPENING PRAYER

Lord, thank you for the sufficiency of your Word. Help me to trust that it has everything I need for a godly life (2 Peter 1:3). Everything I need for life and godliness, for abundant grace and mercy, can be found in the knowledge of Christ set forth in your Word. And everything you require of me is stated in your Word. Thank you for the confidence and freedom this brings, and help me trust your Word as my sufficient guide throughout all my days on earth. Amen.

CHAPTER REVIEW

1. Describe the sufficiency of Scripture in your own words:

2. True / False: It is possible to obey all of Scripture in this life.

3. How can we discern whether the leading of the Spirit today is legitimate?

4. Is it possible to know God's will? Explain your answer.

THINKING CRITICALLY

5. How would you describe the relationship between the sufficiency of Scripture and our ability to teach theology and ethics?

6. Based on the doctrine of the sufficiency of Scripture, how would you respond to someone who is trying to add to the teaching of Scripture?

PERSONAL ENGAGEMENT

7. What role does the Bible play in your assessment of what you should do in any given situation? Do you allow it to be sufficient, or do you primarily seek assurance from other sources?

8. As you close your time in this chapter, thank God for the sufficiency of his Word and how it can be our source of assurance.

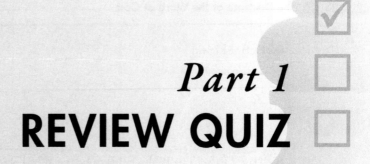

REVIEW QUIZ

1. What are the four characteristics of Scripture?

    1.

    2.

    3.

    4.

2. What is the definition of *systematic theology*? (Circle your answer and label the remaining three options.)

    a. A study of how Christians in different periods have understood various theological topics.

    b. Any study that answers the question, "What does the whole Bible teach us today?" about any given topic.

    c. Studying theological topics using the tools and methods of philosophical reasoning and what can be known about God from observing the universe.

    d. Providing a defense of the truthfulness of the Christian faith for the purpose of convincing unbelievers.

3. Which of the following is *not* one of the options given as a meaning for the phrase "the Word of God"?

    a. Jesus Christ

    b. The Bible

    c. Words of modern-day prophets

    d. God's actual speech

4. Define *canon*:

5. True / False: The Bible claims to be the Word of God.

6. Describe the difference between inerrancy and the precision of Scripture.

7. The clarity of Scripture means that:

    a. The Bible contains nothing that is hard to understand.

    b. The Bible is written in such a way that it is able to be understood.

    c. The Bible is impossible to understand.

    d. The Bible requires advanced degrees to understand.

PART 2

The Doctrine of God

CHAPTER 9

The Existence of God

OPENING PRAYER

Lord, you are! Unlike all the other so-called gods, you exist and are not the invention or projection of human experience. You exist all by yourself, and you have always existed. You still exist even when people deny that you do. You are the source of everything else that exists. Please help me to live out my belief in your existence, and keep me from "practical atheism." Amen.

CHAPTER REVIEW

1. How do we know that God exists?

   a.

   b.

2. How does creation point to the existence of God?

3. Describe one of the traditional arguments for God's existence in your own words.

THINKING CRITICALLY

4. How would you describe the value of proofs for the existence of God to someone who is doubtful about their value?

5. The Bible says that to deny the existence of God is foolish (Ps 14:1). What would be the best way to communicate that truth to a friend who is an atheist?

PERSONAL ENGAGEMENT

6. Have you ever doubted God's existence? What has helped you to trust in the reality of God's existence?

7. End your time in this chapter by thanking God for revealing his existence to you.

CHAPTER 10

The Knowability of God

OPENING PRAYER

Lord, what a joyful and amazing truth that even though you are infinite you reveal yourself to us and you are knowable! Even though I will never fully fathom the depths of even one thing about you, you tell us that we can know you truly, personally, and sufficiently. Give me humble confidence in my pursuit of knowing you so that I may increase in my intimacy with you (Col. 1:10) and your unsearchable greatness (Ps. 145:3). Amen.

CHAPTER REVIEW

1. Define *incomprehensible*:

2. Though we cannot fully know any one thing about God, how is it true that we can truly know things about God?

3. Complete this verse: "This is eternal life, that they _____ you, the only true God, and Jesus Christ whom you have sent" (John 17:3).

THINKING CRITICALLY

4. Write a list of the things you know about God's love. Describe God's love with some other words.

5. Now write things you do not know fully about God's love.

6. The inevitable overlap on these lists shows the knowability and incomprehensibility of God in a beautiful way.

7. Using the information from this chapter, how would you respond to those who think heaven is boring?

PERSONAL ENGAGEMENT

8. How do you respond to the knowledge of God's incomprehensibility? Does it frustrate or excite you?

9. How might an understanding of both God's knowability and incomprehensibility help those you minister to? Come up with a short statement describing the helpfulness of understanding that God is both knowable and incomprehensible.

10. End your time in this chapter by thanking God that you can know him truly and that you will never know him fully.

THEOLOGICAL EXERCISE

Read Psalm 103 and write down every attribute (characteristic) of God that you can find in the passage.

CHAPTER 11

The Character of God: "Incommunicable" Attributes

OPENING PRAYER

Lord, show me the beauty of your complex and multifaceted nature through your attributes. There is no one like you, for you are the one true God. But you have made us in your likeness and called us to be godly and to reflect your character as the Spirit transforms us from one degree of glory to another. Please help me to know you more deeply as I ponder your character, and give me a healthy, holy fear of you. May I honor you with who I am and how I live. In your mighty, good name I pray. Amen.

CHAPTER REVIEW

1. Define the following terms and give examples of each:

Incommunicable attributes:

Communicable attributes:

2. Why are the categories of incommunicable and communicable ultimately imperfect in their description of these characteristics of God in relation to us?

3. Fill in the blank: In the Bible, a person's _____ is a description of his or her character.

4. Define *anthropomorphic*:

5. True / False: Scripture tells us everything about God's character.

6. Define *independence*:

7. Fill in the blanks: God is _____ in his being, perfections, purposes, and promises, yet God does _____ and _____ emotions, and he acts and feels _____ in response to different situations.

8. Describe and/or illustrate God's relationship to time.

9. What does Jesus' use of the phrase "I am" imply?

10. Define *omnipresence*:

11. Fill in the blanks: Unity: God is not _____ into parts, yet we see _____ attributes of God _____ at different times.

THINKING CRITICALLY

12. Pick one of God's incommunicable attributes, and look it up in a Bible dictionary. In what ways did your understanding of that attribute change or deepen after reading the definition?

13. How does Grudem explain the phenomenon of God "changing his mind" in Scripture? Do you agree or disagree with his assessment?

14. Define *process theology*. What aspects of God's character, outlined by Grudem, does this position miss? Respond to this position in two to three sentences.

PERSONAL ENGAGEMENT

15. Do you praise God for how he is different from you? How could you begin to build this concept into your prayer life?

16. Which aspect of God do you appreciate more easily, his infinity or his personal nature? Ask God to help you have a healthy and balanced view of both.

17. As you finish this chapter, thank God that he created you and determined that you would be meaningful to him.

CHAPTER 12

The Character of God: "Communicable" Attributes (Part 1)

OPENING PRAYER

Lord, you are gracious, kind, loving, merciful, wise, patient, and good. Teach me to see you in the ways that I am like you, and continue to transform me to be more like you. I am made in your image and commanded to reflect that image in my life. Help me, Father, to bear the fruit of the Spirit and to be conformed to the image of Christ in ways that give others a glimpse of who you are so that they will praise your holy name. Amen.

CHAPTER REVIEW

1. What are the five major categories of God's "communicable" attributes?

    1.

    2.

    3.

    4.

    5.

2. Match the following attributes with their definitions:

    a. Spirituality   *b. Invisibility*   *c. Wisdom*   *d. Truthfulness*

    _____ God's total essence, all of his spiritual being, will never be able to be seen by us, yet God still shows himself to us partially in this age and more fully in the age to come.

    _____ God is the true God, and all his knowledge and words are both true and the final standard of truth.

_____ God always chooses the best goals and the best means to those goals.

_____ God exists as a being that is not made of any matter, has no parts or dimensions, is unable to be perceived by our bodily senses, and is more excellent than any other kind of existence.

3. Why is spirituality considered a "communicable" attribute of God?

4. True / False: No one has ever seen an outward manifestation of God.

5. Define *theophany*:

6. Fill in the blanks: Knowledge (Omniscience): God fully _____ himself and all things _____ and _____ in one simple and _____ act.

7. How does Grudem explain the "fear of the Lord"?

8. Define *faithfulness*:

9. How would God be far less good if he were not wrathful?

10. Fill in the blanks: We imitate God's truthfulness when we _____ truth and _____ falsehood.

11. Match the following attributes with their definitions:

a. Goodness   *b. Love*   *c. Mercy*   *d. Grace*   *e. Patience*

_____ God's goodness toward those who deserve only punishment.

_____ God eternally gives of himself to others.

_____ God's goodness toward those in misery and distress.

_____ God is the final standard of good, and all that God is and does is worthy of approval.

_____ God's goodness in withholding of punishment toward those who sin over a period of time.

12. How do we imitate God's love?

13. What is the source of living of the Christian life?

14. Match the following attributes with their definitions:

a. Holiness   *b. Peace*   *c. Righteousness/Justice*   *d. Jealousy*   *e. Wrath*

_____ In God's being and in his actions, he is separate from all confusion and disorder, yet he is continually active in innumerable well-ordered, fully controlled, simultaneous actions.

_____ God continually seeks to protect his honor.

_____ God is separated from sin and devoted to seeking his honor.

_____ God intensely hates all sin.

_____ God always acts in accordance with what is right and is himself the final standard of what is right.

15. How is God's holiness both relational and moral?

16. What is righteousness?

THINKING CRITICALLY

17. Read Psalm 139. Which of God's communicable attributes do you see reflected in this Psalm? Write down each one and define it in the context of this psalm.

18. Define *open theism*. Come up with a two- to four-sentence response to open theism based on your knowledge of the Bible and the content of this chapter.

PERSONAL ENGAGEMENT

19. Consider the truth that "to look at God changes us and makes us like him." How can you more regularly set your gaze upon the Lord?

20. Have you ever praised God for his wrath? How could you put that into practice in your life of prayer and worship?

21. As you finish this chapter, thank God that the knowledge of him can quiet your discouragement, for you can know that he is working wisely in your life, even today, to bring you into greater conformity to the image of Christ.

The Character of God: "Communicable" Attributes (Part 2)

OPENING PRAYER

Lord, continue to help me know you better through a study of your attributes, that I might further love you for all that you are. Help me learn to love everything about you, especially the things that are hard for me to easily like or understand. Please increase my hunger to know you, and give me the discipline, diligence, and focus to seek you more each day. Amen.

CHAPTER REVIEW

1. Match each attribute with its definition:

    a. Will   *b. Freedom*   *c. Omnipotence*   *d. Perfection*

  _____ The attribute of God whereby he does whatever he pleases.

  _____ The attribute of God whereby he approves and determines to bring about every action necessary for the existence and activity of himself and all creation.

  _____ God completely possesses all excellent qualities and lacks no part of any qualities that would be desirable for him.

  _____ God is able to do all his holy will.

2. True / False: Christians sometimes suffer according to God's will.

3. What is the difference between God's necessary will and his free will?

4. Describe the difference between God's secret will and his revealed will.

5. True / False: God can do anything. Explain.

6. How can we imitate God's blessedness?

7. Match each attribute with its definition:

a. Blessedness   *b. Beauty*   *c. Glory*

_____ The created brightness that surrounds God's revelation of himself.

_____ God delights fully in himself and in all that reflects his character.

_____ The attribute of God whereby he is the sum of all desirable qualities.

8. Fill in the blank: God's beauty is closely related to God's _____.

THINKING CRITICALLY

9. Why might suffering be a part of God's will for Christians?

PERSONAL ENGAGEMENT

10. How does further knowledge of God's will through this chapter help you think better about God's will for your life? How has your thinking on God's will been changed?

11. Pick one of God's attributes described in the past two chapters and write a hymn of praise to God centered on that attribute.

12. Close your time in this chapter by thanking God for a particular one of his communicable attributes that has been especially meaningful for you.

Match each attribute with its definition:

1. Independence
2. Unchangeableness/Immutability
3. Eternity
4. Omnipresence
5. Unity
6. Spirituality
7. Invisibility
8. Knowledge (Omniscience)
9. Wisdom
10. Truthfulness/Faithfulness
11. Goodness
12. Love
13. Mercy
14. Grace
15. Patience
16. Holiness
17. Peace/Order
18. Righteousness/Justice
19. Jealousy
20. Wrath
21. Will
22. Freedom
23. Omnipotence (Power/Sovereignty)
24. Perfection
25. Blessedness
26. Beauty
27. Glory

_____ God has no beginning, end, or succession of moments in his own being, and he sees all time equally vividly, yet God sees events and acts in time.

_____ God is able to do all his holy will.

_____ God intensely hates all sin.

_____ God delights fully in himself and in all that reflects his character.

_____ In God's being and in his actions, he is separate from all confusion and disorder, yet he is continually active in innumerable well-ordered, fully controlled, simultaneous actions.

_____ God's total essence, all of his spiritual being, will never be able to be seen by us, yet God still shows himself to us partially in this age and more fully in the age to come.

_____ God is the final standard of good, and all God is and does is worthy of approval.

_____ God's goodness toward those in misery and distress.

_____ God continually seeks to protect his own honor.

_____ God does not need us or the rest of creation for anything, yet we and the rest of creation can glorify him and bring him joy.

_____ God approves and determines to bring about every action necessary for the existence and activity of himself and all creation.

_____ The created brightness that surrounds God's revelation of himself.

_____ God exists as a being that is not made of any matter, has no parts or dimensions, is unable to be perceived by our bodily senses, and is more excellent than any other kind of existence.

_____ God completely possesses all excellent qualities and lacks no part of any qualities that would be desirable for him.

_____ God is the sum of all desirable qualities.

_____ God's goodness in withholding of punishment toward those who sin over a period of time.

_____ God always chooses the best goals and the best means to those goals.

_____ God does not have size or spatial dimensions and is present at every point of space with his whole being, yet God acts differently in different places.

_____ God's goodness toward those who deserve only punishment.

_____ God eternally gives of himself to others.

_____ God does whatever he pleases.

_____ God fully knows himself and all things actual and possible in one simple and eternal act.

_____ God is unchanging in his being, perfections, purposes, and promises, yet God does act and feel emotions, and he acts and feels differently in response to different situations.

_____ God is separated from sin and devoted to seeking his own honor.

_____ God is the true God, and all his knowledge and words are both true and the final standard of truth.

_____ God is not divided into parts, yet we see different attributes of God emphasized at different times.

_____ God always acts in accordance with what is right and is himself the final standard of what is right.

See this workbook's appendix for a complete list of all the attributes with their definitions.

CHAPTER 14

God in Three Persons: The Trinity

OPENING PRAYER

Father, Son, and Holy Spirit, thank you for the unified diversity of your character. Help me to understand this mystery of yourself revealed in Scripture. Father, you sent your Son, and the Spirit brought about the incarnation and empowered Jesus to accomplish his work to redeem lost sinners. The gospel would not be the gospel if you were not who you are as the one God in three persons. Help me to grow in my understanding of the Trinity so that I can understand your redeeming work better as well. Amen.

CHAPTER REVIEW

1. Fill in the blanks: _____ of God's attributes are _____ of all three persons, for each is fully _____.

2. True / False: The word *Trinity* is found throughout the Bible.

3. Why is there more explicit teaching about the Trinitarian nature of God in the New Testament than the Old Testament?

4. What are the three statements that summarize the biblical teaching on the Trinity?

    1.

    2.

    3.

5. How do the specific roles of the persons of the Trinity point to their distinction?

6. What about the Holy Spirit can we learn because of his name being mentioned along with the Father and the Son?

7. True / False: The Bible uses analogies to describe the Trinity.

8. Beside each heresy, put the number corresponding to the statement about the Trinity it denies:

1. God is three persons.   _____ Adoptionism

2. Each person is fully God.   _____ Modalism

3. There is one God.   _____ Subordinationism

_____ Tritheism

_____ Arianism

9. Define *modalism/Sabellianism/modalistic monarchianism*:

10. Define *Arianism*:

11. Define *subordinationism*:

12. Define *adoptionism*:

13. What led to the split between Western and Eastern Christianity? (Circle your answer.)

    Arianism   *adoptionism*   *the filioque clause*   *the Apostles' Creed*   *modalism*

14. Define *tritheism*:

15. Why is the doctrine of the Trinity so important to the church and the Christian faith?

16. Define *economy of the Trinity*:

17. Draw a line between the person of the Trinity and their role(s) in creation and redemption:

God the Father   Accomplished redemption

God the Son   Spoke creative words

God the Holy Spirit   Applies redemption

                                            Sustained God's presence in creation

                                            Carried out creative decrees

                                            Planned redemption

18. What are some of the reasons that the literal meaning of *monogenēs* should be used in the Bible?

19. Give a brief definition of the eternal generation of the Son in your own words:

20. True / False: The distinctions between the persons of the Trinity have to do with their divine nature.

21. Fill in the blanks: The pattern of Father-Son interaction in Scripture is _____, _____ the Father and _____ the Son.

22. Explain the difference between "being" and "person" as described by Grudem.

THINKING CRITICALLY

23. Compare and contrast how the Old Testament reveals the Trinitarian nature of God versus how the New Testament reveals the Trinity.

24. Why is the Jehovah's Witnesses' position on the translation of John 1:1 inconsistent? Write a two- to three-sentence statement refuting this position using biblical evidence.

25. Grudem, in this edition of *Systematic Theology*, explains why he changed his mind on the right translation and meaning of the word *monogenēs* in Scripture. When is it appropriate to change one's mind on issues such as these? How should such a change be approached?

26. Why might those who hold to a feminist view of male-female relationships have issue with the eternal subordination of the Son to the Father?

27. Read the appendix to chapter 14, "Christianity and Mormonism." Pick two of the ten points, and respond to them with concise, biblically founded statements.

PERSONAL ENGAGEMENT

28. How do you relate to each person of the Trinity? Is there one whom you tend to focus on or one whom you often neglect? Ask God to help you relate to him rightly, appreciating both the equality and distinctions of the persons of the Trinity.

29. How does the existence of relationship within the Trinity help you relate to God? How does it teach you the importance of human relationships?

30. End this chapter by thanking God for his mysterious triune nature.

CHAPTER 15

Creation

OPENING PRAYER

Almighty Maker of heaven and earth, all of creation declares your glory. Worship is the only right response when we ponder the work of your hands. Teach me to appreciate your creativity, and let that which you have created point me to greater worship of you. Amen.

CHAPTER REVIEW

1. Define the *doctrine of creation*:

2. *Ex nihilo* is Latin for (circle the correct answer):

Annihilationism   *Out of nothing*   *Out of air*   *Without error*

3. Fill in the blanks: The phrase "the heavens and the earth" includes the _____ _____.

4. True / False: The Bible teaches that God created Adam and Eve in a special and personal way.

5. How is God distinct from his creation?

6. Define *transcendent* and *immanent*:

7. Describe pantheism and how it differs from the biblical view of creation.

8. Define the following terms:

Dualism:

Deism:

9. What does creation primarily show us about God?

10. Fill in the blanks: When all the _____ are _____ understood, there will be "____ _____ _____" between Scripture and natural science.

11. What are some different ways the word *evolution* is used? Define each.

12. Fill in the blanks: "Our culture is exceptional, even _____, by any standard of the _____ kingdom."

13. For something to be pure "creation," it needs to begin (circle one):

from existing matter   from nothing   from a crafting kit

14. Define *theistic evolution*:

15. What does "very good" in the eyes of a holy God imply?

16. How does Romans 1 show the significance of what people believe about God based on creation?

17. True / False: There are gaps in biblical genealogies.

18. Explain the "concordist," or day-age, view:

19. How would a proponent of the framework view suggest that we read Genesis 1?

THINKING CRITICALLY

20. Describe how the biblical worldview regarding creation is different from the view of materialism.

21. How should the relationship between science and Scripture be understood?

22. Explain the concept that "human intuition correctly recognizes that evolution is impossible" with another example.

23. Based on your reading in this chapter, do you lean more toward a young earth or old earth understanding? Explain why.

PERSONAL ENGAGEMENT

24. In what ways do you (or don't you) live as a "practical" materialist?

25. How does the knowledge that there will be no final conflict between Scripture and natural science encourage you?

26. Has the theory of evolution posed an issue for you in regard to your belief in a creator God? How has this chapter helped you in your faith in the teaching of the Bible regarding creation?

27. How should a right understanding of creation help your worship of God?

28. End your study of this chapter by thanking God for his creative work in the world.

God's Providence

OPENING PRAYER

Lord, thank you for your sustaining control over all things in this world. Help me to see your hand at work and worship you more fully through this knowledge. Nothing happens outside of your wise, powerful, guiding hand. Help me to understand all that happens, even sin and evil, as part of your sovereign wisdom, and as a result may I grow in peace, gratitude, and hope. In Jesus' name I pray. Amen.

CHAPTER REVIEW

1. Define *providence*:

God is

    1.

    2.

    3.

2. God's preservation of his creation includes all but which of the following:

    a. God gives us breath each moment.

    b. Christ holds all things together.

    c. God continuously creates new things for every moment.

    d. We have our being in God.

3. How does God's providence provide a basis for science?

4. Describe how weather shows God's concurrence:

5. True / False: Rolling dice falls outside of God's control.

6. Fill in the blanks: All our _____ are under God's providential _____.

7. Do we really cause events to happen? Explain your position.

8. True / False: God is involved in evil things happening and yet bears no moral blame.

9. Complete the verse: Genesis 50:20, "You meant evil against me, but God . . ."

10. Who bears the moral blame for evil actions?

11. Fill in the blanks: There are things that are _____ for God to do but _____ for us to do.

12. How are we free "in the greatest sense"?

13. Define the following terms:

Libertarian free will:

Freedom of inclination:

Compare and contrast the two:

14. What is the difference between God's "moral/revealed will" and his "providential government/ secret will"?

15. Fill in the blanks: The decrees of God are the _____ _____ of God whereby, before the _____ of the world, he _____ to bring about everything that happens.

16. How is the doctrine of the decrees of God distinct from the doctrine of providence?

    a. The doctrine of the decrees of God speaks of his providential actions in time.

    b. The doctrine of the decrees of God speaks about God's decisions before the world was created.

    c. The doctrine of the decrees of God speaks of God's law in condemning sin.

17. What is one very significant means of ours that God has ordained to bring about results in this world? (Circle the correct answer.)

    Sin   *Feats of strength*   *Prayer*   *Faith*   *Wisdom*

18. State the Arminian position on God's providence:

19. True / False: Scripture seems to maintain that choices ordained by God can be real choices.

20. What do Calvinists and Arminians agree on regarding our actions?

21. What are the two positions' major differences?

22. Describe the middle knowledge or Molinist view:

23. True / False: There is no such thing as luck or chance.

THINKING CRITICALLY

24. How might a Calvinist define *free* as it relates to humans and their actions?

25. How might an Arminian understand God's sovereignty as it relates to humans and their actions?

Chapter 16: God's Providence   69

PERSONAL ENGAGEMENT

26. How does a biblical view of providence change your perspective of "ordinary" things like gasoline making your car run? How can you practice worshipful wonder at God's providential work in your life?

27. What is it like to know that we are responsible for our actions and that they have real and eternally significant results? Is that motivating, or does it make you fearful?

28. End your time in this chapter by asking God to help you understand his providence and by praising him for it.

CHAPTER 17

Miracles

OPENING PRAYER

Lord, help me see your wonder-working majesty (Ex. 15:11) and praise you for it. You are the creator and sustainer of all that is, and you have never ceased working in creation. Thank you for always being in the things we take for granted and also for displaying your magnificent power through miracles. Help me to be grateful for your work, whether it is daily or dramatic. Amen.

CHAPTER REVIEW

1. Define *miracle*:

2. Why is the definition "an event impossible to explain by natural causes" insufficient?

3. True / False: Answers to prayer can be miracles.

4. What are the purposes of miracles?

    a.

    b.

    c.

    d.

    e.

5. Who performed miracles in the Bible? Keep a running list as you read through the chapter.

6. What do cessationists believe?

7. Why can the "signs of a true apostle" in 2 Corinthians 12:12 not merely be miracles?

8. What is Geisler's position on miracles?

9. True / False: No one is able to do miracles by a power other than God.

10. Which of the following are proper reasons to ask God to perform a miracle today? (Circle all that apply.)

    a. To bring glory to God

    b. To be entertained

    c. To confirm the truthfulness of the gospel message

    d. To advance one's own power

    e. To remove hindrances to people's ministries

    f. To criticize those who preach the gospel

    g. To help those in need

THINKING CRITICALLY

11. What do you find to be the most helpful critique of Geisler's restrictive definition of miracles? Restate it in your own words, and explain how it denies or complicates Geisler's position.

PERSONAL ENGAGEMENT

12. Before reading this chapter, how would you have defined *miracle*? Now that you have read it, has anything changed about your perspective on miracles?

13. How does your understanding of miracles affect your prayer life? Are you willing to ask God to work miraculously in your life?

14. End your time in this chapter by thanking God for working miraculously in this world and in your life.

CHAPTER 18

Prayer

OPENING PRAYER

Lord, what a great and awesome privilege to come into your presence in prayer. I know that this is only possible because of the finished work of Christ. Please help me to be a more prayerful person and rehearse the gospel every time I enter into your presence. Give me the proper humility and confidence as I pray, and help me to more fully draw near to you. Amen.

CHAPTER REVIEW

1. Define *prayer*:

2. Fill in the blanks: God wants us to pray because prayer expresses our _____ in God and is a means whereby our _____ in him can increase.

3. How is prayer related to wholeness?

4. What three reasons does Grudem state for why God wants us to pray?

    1.

    2.

    3.

5. True / False: Prayer actually changes how God acts in the world.

6. Who makes our prayer effective?

7. Where do we enter with Christ as our Mediator?

8. When following the biblical model, to whom should we primarily direct our prayers?

9. What does it mean to "pray in the Holy Spirit," according to Grudem?

10. How can one increase the depth, power, and wisdom of his or her prayers?

11. Why does Grudem say that listening to God in prayer is important?

12. Where does assured faith in prayer come from? (Circle the correct answer.)

God   *Self-assurance*   *Emotions*   *The universe*   *Our parents*

13. True / False: God only answers the prayers of sinless people. Explain.

14. Fill in the blanks: _____ of sins is necessary in order for God to "_____ us" in the sense of restoring his _____-___-_____ relationship with us.

15. How is God's jealousy related to humility in prayer?

16. Circle all the words that have to do with faithful prayer.

Persistent	Patient	Forgiveness
Earnest	Proud	Sporadic

17. In what ways does a lack of forgiveness hinder prayer?

18. What is the proper place for emotions in prayer?

19. Why pray in private?

20. What are some of the benefits of fasting?

21. Fill in the blank: When prayer remains unanswered, we must continue to _____ God.

THINKING CRITICALLY

22. Grudem mentions modeling good theology in prayer. Why is it important to model what it means to pray "in Jesus' name" in various ways to others in our public prayers?

23. Write a succinct two- to three-sentence statement that would help you explain unanswered prayer to someone who is asking you about it.

PERSONAL ENGAGEMENT

24. Assess your prayer life. Is prayer something you engage in often? Why or why not?

25. How would truly praying in Jesus' name change your prayer life?

26. As you read Grudem's analogy of inviting a friend to dinner, which invitation characterizes the majority of your prayers? Ask God to help you pray expectantly and patiently.

27. As you end this chapter, thank the Lord for the gift of prayer, and ask him to grow you in praying in faith.

Angels

OPENING PRAYER

Thank you, Lord, that you have created your angelic messengers to worship and represent you as well as to minister to your people. Thank you that they even ministered to Jesus during his time on earth. Lord of Hosts, I praise you and join with the hosts of heaven in worshiping you (Neh. 9:6). Amen.

CHAPTER REVIEW

1. Define *angels*:

2. True / False: Angels are spiritual beings.

3. Circle all of the other terms used for angels in Scripture:

Holy ones	Watchers	Principalities
Sons of God	Thrones	Authorities
Spirits	Dominions	
Ministering presence	Invisible friend	

4. Compare and contrast what we know about the cherubim and seraphim:

5. What biblical language speaks of a rank and order among the angels?

6. True / False: Specific convincing scriptural support exists for the concept of individual guardian angels.

7. List what we know about "the angel of the LORD."

8. What are some of the primary ways that we are distinct from angels?

9. How do angels testify to the reality of the unseen world?

10. Name some biblical examples of angels glorifying God.

11. True / False: We need to be cautious of receiving false doctrine from "angels."

12. Why should we not pray to angels?

THINKING CRITICALLY

13. Some people speak of us turning into angels when we die. How might you respond to that statement after reading this chapter? Use Scripture to support your response.

PERSONAL ENGAGEMENT

14. Grudem gave several ways that angels are examples for us. What is one of those areas that you feel you most need to grow in? Ask God for his help in this area.

15. How does it encourage you to know that you are joining in a heavenly throng of worship when you worship?

16. End your time in this chapter by thanking God for what he has revealed in his Word regarding angels, and ask for his help in understanding the role of angels and for his angelic protection in your life.

CHAPTER 20

Satan and Demons

OPENING PRAYER

Lord, thank you that the powers of darkness will not ultimately triumph. But I know that Satan prowls around like a roaring lion seeking to destroy your work and your people. Please enable me to take this fight seriously but never to fear him. Help me to be confident in the power of Christ over everything. Protect me by your Spirit as I seek to understand what your Word teaches about demons. May your Spirit be the only power at work in my life. Amen.

CHAPTER REVIEW

1. Define *demons*:

2. What does 2 Peter 2:4 tell us about "fallen" angels?

3. Who is Satan? What does the term *Satan* mean?

4. True / False: Satan sinned before any human beings did so.

5. What are demons limited by?

6. What can demons *not* do?

7. In the Old Testament, demonic forces are referred to as (circle the correct answer):

False gods   *Demons*   *Angels*   *Satan's armies*   *Hosts*

8. What shift happens in regard to demonic forces from the Old Testament to the New Testament?

9. When will the judgment of Satan and his demons be complete?

10. True / False: All evil is from Satan and demons.

11. Should the primary focus of our evangelistic efforts be on spiritual warfare? Why or why not?

12. True / False: There is no degree of demonic influence in sin and wrongdoing that occurs today.

13. Who bears the primary responsibility of sin in the cases where sin is influenced by demonic powers? Explain.

14. Why does Grudem prefer not to use the term *demon possessed*?

15. Can Christians be influenced by demons? Explain.

16. What is Grudem referring to when he speaks of "spiritual perception"? Give examples.

17. Who has authority to rebuke demons and command them to leave? (Circle the correct answer.)

All people   *Pastors*   *Spiritual warfare experts*   *All Christians*

18. Why might God ask Christians to speak directly to a demon to rebuke it? Give other examples of when God desires our direct involvement and activity in what is ultimately his work.

19. According to Jesus, what ought we to rejoice in rather than our power over demons?

THINKING CRITICALLY

20. Why do Jesus and his followers have power over the demonic that has not been seen before? Explain this in light of the stages of the story of redemption set forth in the Bible.

21. Why do some deny the reality of the spiritual world today? Give biblical examples to bolster an argument for the reality of spiritual activity today.

PERSONAL ENGAGEMENT

22. Before reading this chapter, what was your understanding of spiritual warfare? How has your understanding changed?

23. Do you think there are any areas in your life in which spiritual oppression might be happening? Pray and ask God to help you discern this, and then follow the steps outlined in this chapter to declare your authority in these areas.

24. End your time in this chapter by thanking God for his power over all things and the authority he has given you in Christ over spiritual forces.

1. True / False: We will one day fully understand God.

2. Match the following attributes with their definitions:

1. Independence
2. Eternity
3. Knowledge (Omniscience)

4. Goodness
5. Righteousness/Justice
6. Glory

_____ God has no beginning, end, or succession of moments in his own being, and he sees all time equally vividly, yet God sees events in time and acts in time.

_____ God is the final standard of good, and all that God is and does is worthy of approval.

_____ The created brightness that surrounds God's revelation of himself.

_____ God does not need us or the rest of creation for anything, yet we and the rest of creation can glorify him and bring him joy.

_____ God always acts in accordance with what is right and is himself the final standard of what is right.

_____ God fully knows himself and all things actual and possible in one simple and eternal act.

3. What three statements summarize the biblical teaching on the Trinity?

   1.

   2.

   3.

4. Fill in the blank: God created the universe out of _____.

5. True / False: God is to be blamed for evil.

6. Cessationists are those who believe that:

   a. God stopped creating after day six.

   b. We stopped being independent creatures upon conversion.

   c. Miraculous activity ceased after the age of the apostles.

   d. Demons have ceased afflicting Christians.

7. True / False: Prayer actually changes the way God acts in the world.

8. Angels are physical / spiritual beings. (Circle the correct answer.)

9. Christians have authority over (circle the correct answers):

    a. Angels

    b. Demons

    c. God

PART 3

The Doctrine of Man in the Image of God

CHAPTER 21

The Creation of Man

OPENING PRAYER

Lord, thank you for creating humanity in your image (Gen. 1:26). I am grateful for the privilege of being your created analogy and for the creation mandate to rule over and subdue the earth and to be fruitful and multiply. Thank you that you blessed Adam and Eve before you commanded them to make the most of the gifts you gave them. Please help me to reflect that image in myself and in others more fully every day. Amen.

CHAPTER REVIEW

1. For what primary purpose did God create humanity?

2. Fill in the blanks: Fullness of joy is found in _____ God and _____ in the excellence of his character.

3. Why is it inappropriate for man to seek glory but wholly appropriate for God to do so?

4. What does it mean to say that man is made in the image of God?

5. Describe the three major views of the image of God as outlined by Millard Erickson:

    1. The substantive view:

    2. The relational view:

    3. The functional view:

6. True / False: The words for *image* and *likeness* in Hebrew imply being identical to God.

7. Which passage in Genesis shows us that man is still created in God's image after the fall?

8. How does Grudem describe the state of the image of God in man after the fall?

    a. Exactly the same

    b. Distorted

    c. Lost

    d. Perfected

    e. Stolen

9. What reality in the New Testament enables us to "progressively grow into more and more likeness to God"?

10. From Romans 8:29, what is the goal for which God has redeemed us?

11. At Christ's return, what will the ultimate state of the image of God be in believers?

12. Given each aspect of the image of God in humanity, define it briefly and then give an example:

Aspects	Definition	Example
Moral Aspects		
Spiritual Aspects		
Mental Aspects		
Relational Aspects		
Physical Aspects		

13. Fill in the blank: We are the _____ of God's infinitely wise and skillful work of creation.

THINKING CRITICALLY

14. How do the differences between humanity and animals described in this chapter bolster the argument against macroevolution?

15. What implications does the doctrine of man being created in the image of God have on the way we operate in interpersonal relationships or in society at large?

PERSONAL ENGAGEMENT

16. How does it help your own understanding of self-worth to know that you are truly important to God for all eternity?

17. Knowing that all human beings are made in the image of God, how will that change how you interact with others? Think of all spheres of life, from those in your immediate family to the checker at the grocery store.

18. As you close your time in this chapter, thank God for creating you, and all people, in his image, and ask him to continue the work of renewing that image in you.

CHAPTER 22

Man as Male and Female

OPENING PRAYER

Lord, thank you for your design of humanity as male and female. Satan hates the way you glorify yourself through humanity as male and female, and there is so much confusion about this in our day. Show me the beauty of gender distinctions as well as the equality of dignity and worth they share. Help me to understand and love what it means to be the gender you created me to be. Amen.

CHAPTER REVIEW

1. What are the three ways the creation as male and female shows God's image?

    1.

    2.

    3.

2. Where does interpersonal unity come to its fullest expression in this age? Explain this unity.

3. Is marriage the only way that interpersonal relationships reflect the nature of the Trinity? Give other examples.

4. Fill in the blank: Men and women have been created by God to be _____ in their importance and personhood.

5. In what ways are men and women equal according to Grudem?

6. Which aspect of this doctrine, according to Grudem, sets Christianity apart from almost all religions and societies and cultures?

7. Compare and contrast the difference in roles between the members of the Trinity and between men and women.

8. Grudem argues that:

  a. Differences in roles between men and women were initiated after the fall.

  b. Differences in roles between men and women were designed by God in the beginning.

  c. Differences in roles between men and women do not exist.

  d. Differences in roles between men and women are a modern social construct.

9. Define *primogeniture*:

10. True / False: Adam naming Eve indicates a leadership role on his part.

11. Who is representative of the human race in their sin, Adam or Eve? (Circle your answer.)

THINKING CRITICALLY

12. What is lost if we deny the understanding and practice of the equality of men and women?

13. What is lost if we deny the distinctions between men and women?

14. Why do you think there is a movement in culture today to do away with distinctions between men and women?

PERSONAL ENGAGEMENT

15. Do you enjoy being your gender? Why or why not?

16. How has this chapter clarified or contradicted what you believe about gender?

17. As you close your time in this chapter, thank God that he makes us male and female, and that he glorifies himself through that.

CHAPTER 23

The Essential Nature of Man

OPENING PRAYER

Lord, thank you for making me body and soul. You created the physical and spiritual realms, you made human beings as physical and spiritual beings, and you declared all of creation as very good. Please help me to understand what it means to honor you with all of who you have made me to be. Amen.

CHAPTER REVIEW

1. Define the following terms:

Monism:

Dichotomy:

Trichotomy:

2. Fill in the blank: A frequent emphasis of Scripture is on the overall _____ of man as created by God.

3. Scripture uses what two words interchangeably?

    a. *Mind* and *spirit*

    b. *Spirit* and *body*

    c. *Soul* and *spirit*

4. Explain Grudem's argument for a dichotomist view of the nature of the immaterial part of humans.

5. Give some biblical examples of what activities our souls do.

6. What are the distinctions between the dichotomist and trichotomist views?

7. How does this discussion relate to our distinction as humans from animals?

8. What does a healthy emphasis on dichotomy within an overall unity remind us about Christian growth?

9. Define the following terms:

Creationism:

Traducianism:

THINKING CRITICALLY

10. Do you agree with Grudem's dichotomist perspective? Why or why not?

PERSONAL ENGAGEMENT

11. How does understanding that you are both body and spirit change your perspective on life?

12. When you think about worship, which aspect of yourself do you tend to engage with more in worship? How can you worship in both "spirit" and "truth" (John 4:23) with your whole self?

13. End your time in this chapter by thanking God for creating you as a holistic person with body and soul.

CHAPTER 24

Sin

OPENING PRAYER

Lord, help me to see my sin for what it is, a grievous attitude and act against you. Help me to seek forgiveness from you and recognize your grace and mercy. You are holy, and we have all rebelled against you, the most high King. But you are gracious, and the Comforter you sent also kindly convicts of sin and brings us to godly sorrow and true repentance. As I study this chapter, please bring me to deeper sorrow for my sin so I can rest more deeply in the magnitude of your grace. Amen.

CHAPTER REVIEW

1. Define *sin*:

2. True / False: Our very nature is sinful.

3. Fill in the blanks: Sin is directly _____ to all that is good in the _____ of God.

4. To blame God for sin would be:

    a. Blasphemy

    b. Just

    c. Unfair

5. What was the first sin, and what three elements did it entail?

6. All sin is ultimately:

    a. Evil

    b. Selfish

    c. Conceivable

    d. Irrational

7. In what two ways do we inherit sin from Adam? Describe each.

8. Define *impute*. Describe how it relates to our sinful nature.

9. True / False: According to Grudem, all sin is ultimately irrational and makes no sense.

10. Does "total depravity," or total inability, mean that we are as bad as we can be? Why or why not?

THINKING CRITICALLY

11. Explain why Grudem prefers the term *inherited* rather than *original*:

12. Do you agree with Grudem's belief that there are degrees of sin? Aren't all sins the same to God? Briefly state your answer and give biblical basis for it.

13. Do you think it's fair that we all inherit a sinful nature? How would you explain inherited sin to someone who thinks God cannot hold us accountable for something we inherit?

PERSONAL ENGAGEMENT

14. Have you ever experienced deep sorrow for your sin? If not, how does considering your sin make you feel now? If you have, where did that sorrow lead you?

15. What are ways you tend to minimize, excuse, or rationalize your sin, or blame your sin on others?

16. The Bible says that although Christ knew no sin, he became sin for us (2 Cor. 5:21). In what ways are you walking in the freedom that brings by faith in him?

17. End your time in this chapter by asking the Lord to forgive you of your sins and thanking him for the forgiveness found in Christ.

CHAPTER 25

The Covenants between God and Man

OPENING PRAYER

Lord, thank you for being a covenant-making and promise-keeping God. Help me relate to you in trust as I understand this aspect of your character more fully. You always do what you say you will. Thank you that although we waver and fail, you never do. Thank you that we can count on you to be true and faithful. Amen.

CHAPTER REVIEW

1. Define *covenant*:

2. What are the two options that humans have in a covenant with God?

    a. Accept

    b. Negotiate

    c. Reject

    d. Change

    e. Rewrite

3. Describe the covenant at play in the garden of Eden. Who was involved, what were the conditions, and what was the promise of blessing?

4. True / False: The covenant of works does not remain in force. Explain.

5. Who is involved in the covenant of redemption, and what roles do they have?

6. Describe the covenant of grace:

Parties:

Condition:

Promise:

Sign:

7. Fill in the following chart based on the information in the chapter on the various forms of the covenant of grace.

Name of Covenant	Key People Involved	Key Passage(s)

THINKING CRITICALLY

8. Compare and contrast covenant theology and dispensationalism. Based on your reading of the Bible and this chapter, how do you see the Old and New Testaments in relation to one another when it comes to how God relates to his people?

PERSONAL ENGAGEMENT

9. How does it encourage you to know that as a believer you are in a covenant with a God who always keeps his promises?

10. As you think about sharing the gospel with others, would it be helpful to include a discussion of covenants in the conversation? Why or why not?

11. Now that you know that you are in a covenant with God, how do you think he is calling you to live as a part of that covenant?

12. As you conclude this chapter, thank God for the covenant that he has made with his people through Jesus.

1. Which of the following *does not* represent a biblical understanding of inherited sin?

    a. Adam was created in a state of holiness and original righteousness.

    b. Adam's fall resulted in the corruption of human nature, which made us all guilty and corrupted at conception.

    c. We are born in a state of original righteousness, and our human nature becomes corrupted only if and when we sin as individuals.

    d. We are guilty before God because of Adam's disobedience.

2. Fill in the blank: God created us for his own _____.

3. In the fall, God's image in man was:

    a. Lost forever

    b. Remained unchanged

    c. Distorted but not lost

    d. Perfected

4. True / False: Men and women are equal in personhood and importance.

5. Trichotomists and dichotomists disagree on:

    a. The role of men and women in the church

    b. The distinction between spirit and soul

    c. Who is held responsible for sin

    d. How to understand the Lord's Supper

6. True / False: God can be blamed for sin.

7. The following is the definition of what word? _____

Failure to conform to the moral law of God in act, attitude, or nature.

8. Which biblical characters had significant covenants made with them in Scripture? (Circle all that apply.)

    a. Adam

    b. Noah

    c. Joshua

    d. Jesus

    e. Abraham

    f. Deborah

    g. Moses

    h. David

    i. Elisha

The Doctrines of Christ and the Holy Spirit

PART 4

The Doctrines of Christ and the Holy Spirit

CHAPTER 26

The Person of Christ

OPENING PRAYER

Lord Jesus, you are the Way, the Truth, and the Life. As I study this chapter, please help me to know you more truly, depend on you more fully, and obey you more faithfully. You became the God-man, joyfully came to a world that hated you, and redeemed us from our lost and hopeless condition. Thank you for being our King and becoming a merciful and faithful high priest and meeting us where we were. I am forever grateful. Amen.

CHAPTER REVIEW

1. Write out Grudem's summary of the biblical teaching about the person of Christ below:

2. How is the virgin birth related to inherited sin?

3. True / False: Jesus had a human body.

4. What emotions did Jesus experience during his life? List a few examples.

5. In what one important respect was Jesus different from any other human in his humanity?

6. Fill in the blanks: Jesus obeyed God _____ as a _____.

7. Define *impeccable*:

8. Why did Jesus have to be fully human? Provide two to three reasons and give scriptural support.

9. Jesus will be a man:

    a. He isn't a man anymore.

    b. Until he comes again

    c. Forever

10. Define *incarnation*:

11. How do we see Jesus displaying divine attributes?

12. The assertion that "Jesus was fully God and fully man in one person" is:

    a. A contradiction

    b. Incoherent

    c. A paradox

    d. Unintelligible

13. Why was it necessary for Jesus to be fully divine? Give 2–3 reasons.

14. Define the following inadequate views of Christ:

Apollinarianism:

Nestorianism:

Monophysitism (Eutychianism):

15. What is meant by the phrase "hypostatic union"?

THINKING CRITICALLY

16. Could Jesus have sinned? Explain your answer.

17. Describe and respond with biblical argumentation to the kenosis theory.

18. Explain how one nature of Christ does things that the other does not.

PERSONAL ENGAGEMENT

19. How does knowing that Jesus obeyed God fully as a man help you when you are tempted by sin?

20. What does it say about God's love that he would come to earth and live and die as a man for you? How would understanding what God did change how you go about your days?

21. As you close your time in this chapter, thank God for the amazing miracle of Jesus becoming man forever to fulfill his plan of redemption.

CHAPTER 27

The Atonement

OPENING PRAYER

Lord Jesus, thank you for the work you have done on my behalf in your life and death to save me. You became one of us so you could save us from ourselves, our sin, and death. Thank you for your obedience in place of my disobedience, for your bearing the wrath and death I deserved. Thank you for the cross and for laying down your life so I could live. Please help me to go much deeper in my understanding of the atonement as I study this chapter. Amen.

CHAPTER REVIEW

1. Define *atonement*:

2. What two attributes of God led to Christ's coming to earth and dying for our sins?

3. Fill in the blanks: Christ's active obedience was Christ's _____ for ____.

4. Why did Jesus need to live a life of perfect obedience for us?

5. Fill in the blanks: Christ's _____ obedience was his _____ for us.

6. True / False: Christ only suffered for us on the cross.

7. What does it mean that God imputed our sin to Christ?

8. Define *propitiation*:

9. Explain the term *penal substitution*:

10. Match the aspect of Christ's death with our need that we have as sinners.

a. Sacrifice

b. Propitiation

c. Reconciliation

d. Redemption

_____ We deserve to bear God's wrath against sin.

_____ We are in bondage to sin and to the kingdom of Satan.

_____ We deserve to die as the penalty for sin.

_____ We are separated from God by our sins.

11. Define the following terms:

Limited atonement:

Unlimited atonement:

THINKING CRITICALLY

12. Explain the respective roles of each member of the Trinity in the atonement.

13. What does Grudem propose as an explanation for 1 Peter 3:19–20? Do you find his proposal persuasive? Why or why not?

14. Which view on the extent of the atonement do you find most compelling? Explain why.

PERSONAL ENGAGEMENT

15. How does knowing that Jesus lived a perfect life and died a sacrificial death on your behalf encourage you in your daily Christian walk?

16. To close your time in this chapter, think about how your life would be without Christ's salvation, and then thank Jesus for his sacrifice, propitiation, reconciliation, and redemption on your behalf.

CHAPTER 28

Resurrection and Ascension

OPENING PRAYER

Dear Lord, please help me to walk in the newness of life that is ours through the resurrection of Christ. Lead me to greater dependence on and confidence in him as my present mediator because he is the ascended Lord. Amen.

CHAPTER REVIEW

1. How was Jesus' resurrected body the same as our bodies now?

2. What are the ways Jesus' resurrected body is different than our bodies now?

3. True / False: Even if Jesus never actually rose from the dead, we should still hold to our beliefs in him.

4. Explain the main things that Christ's resurrection accomplished.

5. Explain the main things the ascension of Christ accomplished.

6. Fill in the blanks: Christ received _____ and _____ that _____ _____ been his before.

7. Fill in the blanks: The two main states of Jesus Christ are _____ and _____.

THINKING CRITICALLY

8. What are the main reasons you believe in the resurrection?

9. How would you respond to someone who says, "My faith in Christ would not change at all even if they found Jesus' body in a grave in Jerusalem tomorrow"?

PERSONAL ENGAGEMENT

10. How important is the resurrection of Christ in your daily life? What are ways the resurrection can help us as we go through tragedies, trials, and disappointments?

11. How does the ascension inform the way you think about your humanity, including your human body?

12. As you conclude your study of this chapter, ask God to help you to experience more resurrection power in your daily life. Pray that your soul would be flooded with great hope because Jesus has conquered death and is coming back one day.

CHAPTER 29

The Offices of Christ

OPENING PRAYER

Lord, please lead me to greater assurance of my salvation when I consider how perfectly Jesus has fulfilled the office of prophet, priest, and king. Thank you that he is the perfect Word, sacrifice, and Lord. Amen.

CHAPTER REVIEW

1. Provide definitions of the three offices of Christ.

Prophet:

Priest:

King:

2. How is Jesus different from all the other prophets before him?

3. How is Jesus different from all the other priests before him?

4. How is Jesus different from all the other kings before him?

5. Describe how the church is to represent Christ in prophetic, priestly, and kingly ways.

THINKING CRITICALLY

6. Given the way Christ has fulfilled the offices of prophet, priest, and king, how should this shape the way we read and interpret the Old Testament?

7. What is the relationship between Jesus as the true and perfect Prophet, and the belief that the Bible is sufficient and we do not need further additions to it?

PERSONAL ENGAGEMENT

8. Jesus is the true and perfect Prophet, and he said that if we love him we will obey him. How much do you appreciate the vital connection between love and obedience? When you feel love for Christ, are you more motivated to obey him?

9. Does considering that Jesus always lives to intercede for you bring rest to your soul?

10. What are practical ways you can represent Jesus as king in your circles of influence?

11. To close your time in this chapter, thank God for his perfect plan of redemption and for the knowledge that there is nothing we need to add to Christ's work on our behalf.

CHAPTER 30

The Work of the Holy Spirit

OPENING PRAYER

Dear Lord, thank you for sending the precious Holy Spirit, just as you promised. Thank you for the wonderful way he comforts us, convicts us of sin, enlightens our minds, bears fruit in our lives, and transforms us into the image of Christ. Amen.

CHAPTER REVIEW

1. Define the work of the Holy Spirit:

2. Fill in the blanks: The Holy Spirit is now the _____ manifestation of the presence of the _____ among us. He is the one who is most prominently _____ with us now.

3. Name the four ways the Spirit brings evidence of God's presence and blessing, and give an example of each:

    1.

    2.

    3.

    4.

4. What are some ways in which the Holy Spirit brings about holiness in our lives?

5. How did the Spirit work in the Old Testament?

6. Define "blasphemy against the Holy Spirit" using the context of the passages in which it is mentioned (Matt. 12:22–32; Mark 3:22–30).

THINKING CRITICALLY

7. As you consider the teaching of Scripture regarding the Holy Spirit, what are some ways to discern whether the Spirit is the one leading you?

PERSONAL ENGAGEMENT

8. How often do you think about the Holy Spirit's work in your life?

9. Have you practiced walking by the Spirit? What things could you place in your life to remind you of your dependence on the Spirit?

10. As you close your time in this chapter, thank the Lord for his work in your life through the power of the Holy Spirit, and ask him to continue that work in greater measure.

1. Fill in the blanks: Jesus Christ was fully _____ and fully _____ in one _____, and he will be so forever.

2. True / False: Jesus was only sinless because he was divine.

3. The incarnation refers to:

    a. Jesus dying on the cross

    b. Jesus descending into hell

    c. Jesus coming to earth as a man

    d. Jesus going up to heaven

4. True / False: Jesus' only act for our salvation was his perfect substitutionary death.

5. What is meant by the term *penal substitution*?

    a. Jesus' death bore the penalty for us in our place.

    b. Jesus' death was a penalty for coming to earth as a human.

    c. Jesus' death paid the ransom for our sins.

    d. Jesus died as our example.

6. True / False: Jesus will be human forever.

7. Where is Jesus now?

8. What are the three offices of Christ? Define each.

   1.

   2.

   3.

9. What is one of the primary activities of the Holy Spirit in our lives?

   a. Redeeming us

   b. Sanctifying us

   c. Choosing us

   d. Loving us

10. True / False: The Holy Spirit was not active in the Old Testament.

The Doctrine of the Application of Redemption

CHAPTER 31

Common Grace

OPENING PRAYER

Lord, thank you that you are always revealing yourself and providing for your creation. Help me to be more aware of your common grace at work and have a heart filled with gratitude because of it. Amen.

CHAPTER REVIEW

1. Define *common grace*:

2. How is the manifestation of "saving grace" different from "common grace"?

3. Fill in the blanks: The goodness that is found in the whole _____ is due to God's _____ and _____.

4. True / False: Science and technology carried out by non-Christians is not a result of God's grace.

5. How does the restraint of evil show common grace?

6. Does God ever answer the prayers of unbelievers? Explain.

7. Does common grace save people? Explain.

8. What are the four reasons that God bestows common grace?

1.

2.

3.

4.

THINKING CRITICALLY

9. What is the relationship between common grace and the unbeliever?

PERSONAL ENGAGEMENT

10. How does a greater understanding of God's common grace change the way you engage with the things around you created by humans?

11. Have you ever thought about the concept of common grace before? How does understanding common grace help you see more fully God's activity in the world?

12. As you close your time in this chapter, thank God for his common grace that is extended to the whole world, and ask him to help you see his grace more clearly every day.

CHAPTER 32

Election and Reprobation

OPENING PRAYER

Lord, I am grateful that you are the sovereign king of creation and that nothing happens outside your wise providence. Thank you for your sovereign grace that can never be earned. Help me to rest in your complete knowledge, goodness, and love. Amen.

CHAPTER REVIEW

1. Election is chronologically the _____ of God's dealing with us in a gracious way.

    a. End

    b. Outcome

    c. Beginning

    d. Foundation

2. Place in order and briefly define each of the following elements of "the order of salvation."

Election	1.
The gospel call	2.
Regeneration	3.
Conversion	4.
Justification	5.
Adoption	6.
Sanctification	7.
Perseverance	8.
Death	9.
Glorification	10.

3. Define *election*:

4. List a few of the key passages relating to election.

5. True / False: The doctrine of election is provided to instill fear in nonbelievers.

6. What type of knowledge is meant by God "knowing" someone in passages like 1 Corinthians 8:3?

7. Grudem concludes that election is:

    a. Conditional

    b. Unconditional

8. Compare and contrast "libertarian free will / absolutely free will" and "freedom of inclination."

9. True / False: It would be perfectly fair for God not to save anyone.

10. Define *reprobation*:

11. Fill in the blanks: In the presentation of Scripture the _____ of election lies in God, and the _____ for reprobation lies in the sinner.

THINKING CRITICALLY

12. Some consider the doctrine of election to be a reason not to engage in evangelism. How would you argue against this view using Scripture and what you have learned from this chapter?

13. Evaluate the view known as "middle knowledge." What are the strongest points regarding middle knowledge? What are its weaknesses?

PERSONAL ENGAGEMENT

14. Have you ever considered the doctrine of election as a reason to praise God? How has this chapter helped shape your understanding of this doctrine as a praiseworthy thing?

15. There are many portions of this doctrine that may cause discomfort for you. When you are faced with those feelings of discomfort, how do they change your attitude toward God and his Word? Ask God to help you be taught by him and his Word, even in areas of discomfort or confusion.

16. As you close your time in this chapter, thank God for deciding to set his love on those who have called on his name, and praise him for his glorious grace.

CHAPTER 33

The Gospel Call and Effective Calling

OPENING PRAYER

Heavenly Father, thank you that you take the initiative in bringing your people to yourself through your sovereign grace. Help me to be a faithful witness for you, because no one is beyond your reach. Amen.

CHAPTER REVIEW

1. Define *effective calling*:

2. True / False: People will be saved by the power of the effective call apart from their own willing response to the gospel.

3. What is the external/general calling? How is it distinct from the effective call?

4. What are the three important elements of the gospel call?

    1.

    2.

    3.

5. In addition to agreeing to the above statements, what else is needed for a person to be saved?

6. What two things are often mentioned together when the Bible speaks of conversion?

    a. Faith

    b. Works

    c. Repentance

    d. Obedience

THINKING CRITICALLY

7. Why do you think the call of God follows predestination and leads to justification? Do you think the order could be different? Why or why not?

8. How do you think the preaching of the gospel by a human being and the call of God work together?

PERSONAL ENGAGEMENT

9. Have you personally responded to the call of the gospel? If not, what is stopping you from making that decision today? Talk about this with another believer. If you have personally trusted in Jesus, write about that experience below.

10. After reading about the importance of a personal response to the call of the gospel, how does that change how you think about the importance and value of evangelism?

11. As you close your time in this chapter, thank God for the gospel call and your own response to it. Ask him to help you further surrender yourself to Jesus in faith each day.

CHAPTER 34

Regeneration

OPENING PRAYER

Dear Lord, I am deeply grateful that you have the power to bring those who are spiritually dead back to life and that you seek and save those who have turned their backs to you. Please help me to walk in the new life I have in Christ and faithfully share the good news with others who are walking in darkness. Amen.

CHAPTER REVIEW

1. Define *regeneration*:

2. True / False: We play an active role in the work of regeneration in our lives.

3. Which persons of the Trinity are spoken of as being active in the work of regeneration?

4. Does regeneration or effective calling come first? Explain your answer.

5. Is regeneration always an instantaneous event?

6. Which occurs first:

   a. Regeneration

   b. Saving faith

7. What is the solution to spiritual deadness and the human inability to respond to God?

8. What are some of the results of regeneration in the believer?

9. True / False: It is possible for a person to be regenerated and not become truly converted.

THINKING CRITICALLY

10. What does Grudem state as the problem with using the term *irresistible grace*? Do you agree or disagree with his points? What might a more helpful phrase be to describe what is happening?

11. What is the relationship between the doctrine of regeneration and evangelism? How should those doing evangelism think about their role in light of the reality of God's work in regeneration?

PERSONAL ENGAGEMENT

12. What results of regeneration do you see in your life?

13. Do you acknowledge the reality that your regeneration, and the regeneration of others, is a work of God? Why or why not?

14. As you close your time in this chapter, thank God for his work of regeneration in your life.

CHAPTER 35

Conversion (Faith and Repentance)

OPENING PRAYER

Lord, thank you that when we turn from our sin and trust you instead of our useless self-effort, you give us a brand-new start and put us on the path of following in the steps of our Savior. Thank you for the saving power of the Spirit of holiness and the gospel of peace. Amen.

CHAPTER REVIEW

1. Define *conversion*:

2. True / False: Knowledge alone is enough for salvation. Explain.

3. Fill in the blanks: Saving faith is _____ in Jesus Christ as a living person for forgiveness of _____ and for eternal life with God.

4. Explain the three elements that must be present when a person comes to trust in Christ.

5. What is the relationship between knowledge and faith?

6. Define *repentance*:

7. True / False: Genuine repentance can occur before the living of a changed life over a period of time.

8. What does genuine repentance result in?

9. Repentance and faith are:

   a. Two different actions that happen at different times

   b. Completely unrelated

   c. Two sides of the same coin

10. Does repentance primarily mean "to change one's mind"? Explain your answer.

11. Briefly explain some problems put forth by Grudem with the Free Grace teaching regarding saving faith.

12. How does Grudem explain the role of praying a prayer of salvation? Do you agree or disagree?

THINKING CRITICALLY

13. Define faith and contrast the world's use of the word *faith* with the Bible's use of the word *faith*.

14. What would you say are the key differences between true and false repentance?

15. What would happen to our idea of faith if it did not necessarily include repentance?

PERSONAL ENGAGEMENT

16. What role has repentance played in your faith life? Would you say your life is characterized by an attitude of repentance and faith? How can you more regularly walk in repentance?

17. When you share the gospel with others, do you include the idea of repentance? How could you further emphasize the importance of turning from sin when you share the truth of the gospel?

18. To close your time in this chapter, thank God for leading you to repentance, and ask him for his help to continually draw you into greater faith and trust in him.

CHAPTER 36

Justification (Right Legal Standing before God)

OPENING PRAYER

Heavenly Father, you are the judge of all the earth. Thank you that I have been made right with you through the righteousness of Christ. Thank you that in him I will be able to stand before you not only forgiven but justified in your sight. In the name of Jesus, I pray. Amen.

CHAPTER REVIEW

1. What was the primary issue in the Protestant Reformation?

2. Fill in the blanks: Justification is an _____ _____ act of God in which he thinks of our sins as _____ and Christ's _____ as belonging to us, and _____ us to be _____ in his sight.

3. Define the following terms:

Forensic:

Impute:

4. In what other doctrines was there a discussion of imputation? What was imputed and to whom?

5. Define the following terms:

Infused righteousness:

Merit:

6. What is the primary difference between the understanding of justification that Grudem presents and the Roman Catholic understanding?

7. What is the difference between regeneration and justification?

8. Fill in the blanks: Justification comes to us entirely by God's _____, not on account of any _____ in ourselves.

9. Why might faith be the attitude of heart that God chose by which we would obtain justification?

THINKING CRITICALLY

10. If the apostle James says that a person is "justified by works and not by faith alone" (James 2:24), how can it also be true that we are justified by faith alone (Rom. 5:17–19)?

11. How is "Paul's gospel," as presented by N. T. Wright, different from the gospel message outlined by Grudem in earlier chapters?

PERSONAL ENGAGEMENT

12. How is it encouraging to know that the righteousness of Christ is imputed to us? How does understanding that reality change how you think about your Christian walk?

13. What hope does the doctrine of justification offer you and those you minister to?

14. Close your time in this chapter by thanking God for his work of justification and his imputation of Christ's righteousness to those who believe.

CHAPTER 37

Adoption (Membership in God's Family)

OPENING PRAYER

Heavenly Father, thank you that you not only forgive us, but you declare us righteous and even adopt us as your children so that we can cry, "Abba, Father." Please help me to rest in the security that comes with being your child, and give me a heart for the orphans in our world. Amen.

CHAPTER REVIEW

1. Define *adoption*:

2. What evidence is there in the lives of believers that they are God's children?

3. Are we currently fully adopted as children of God? Explain your answer.

4. What does the New Testament connect adoption to?

    a. Regeneration

    b. New birth

    c. Saving faith

    d. Works

5. How is adoption distinct from justification and regeneration?

6. Fill in the blanks: God gives us an _____ witness from the Holy Spirit that causes us _____ to call God our Father.

THINKING CRITICALLY

7. How is discipline a privilege of adoption? What role does discipline play in the Christian life?

8. Do you think there is a connection between God's adoption of his children and the command in James to "look after orphans and widows in their distress" (James 1:27 NIV)?

9. What would be lacking in our relationship with God if we only had forgiveness and justification and not adoption?

PERSONAL ENGAGEMENT

10. When you think of God as Father and of yourself as an adopted child, how does that make you feel? Is it easy or hard to relate to God as Father? Why or why not?

11. How easily do you submit to the Lord's discipline?

12. When others look at your life, would they be able to see the impact on you of being in God's family?

13. Return to the list of privileges of adoption, and to close your time in this chapter, walk through the list and thank God for each and how he has shown you each particularly in your life.

CHAPTER 38

Sanctification (Growth in Likeness to Christ)

OPENING PRAYER

Heavenly Father, thank you for the work of the Spirit in the lives of your people that makes us holy. I pray that I would be set apart more each day and that the fruit of the Spirit would flourish in my life. Amen.

CHAPTER REVIEW

1. Define *sanctification*:

2. What are some key differences between justification and sanctification?

3. Name and describe the three stages of sanctification:

1.

2.

3.

4. What two extremes must we avoid as Christians when it comes to our sin?

5. When is sanctification complete for our souls and bodies? Explain.

6. Describe the perfectionism view.

7. Who cooperates in sanctification?

   a. God

   b. Believers

   c. God and believers

8. Describe both the passive and active roles we play in our sanctification.

THINKING CRITICALLY

9. Hebrews 12:14 says, "Without holiness no one will see the Lord" (NIV). How do you think this condition of knowing God relates to God's sanctifying work in the life of the believer?

10. Grudem defines *sanctification* as a progressive work whereby we become increasingly holier over time. How do you think that definition fits with Hebrews 10:10, which says that "we have been sanctified through the offering of the body of Jesus Christ once for all," which sounds like it has already been accomplished?

11. What do you think are the negative effects of some traditions in the history of the church referring to only a special select few Christians as saints?

PERSONAL ENGAGEMENT

12. Chart your own sanctification progress throughout your life. When did you have significant "high" points? What were some significant "low" points? Process these with the Lord in prayer.

13. Do you see yourself as a saint? If you have trusted Christ for salvation, the Bible says you are a "holy one." How would claiming this title and identity for yourself have an impact on your daily life?

14. To what extent are you participating in the active portion of your sanctification? Ask the Lord to help you in your participation in his work in your life.

15. As you close your time in this chapter, thank God for his work of sanctification in you, and ask him to help you see the beauty and joy of your growth in holiness.

CHAPTER 39

Baptism in and Filling with the Holy Spirit

OPENING PRAYER

Dear heavenly Father, thank you for sending the Spirit to dwell in your people and empower us for life in Christ. Please show me the difference between walking in the flesh and walking in the Spirit, and lead me to a more fruitful life of dependence on him. Amen.

CHAPTER REVIEW

1. True / False: Baptism of the Holy Spirit happens before conversion.

2. Briefly summarize the five ways the traditional Pentecostal view of the baptism of the Holy Spirit is supported:

    1.

    2.

    3.

    4.

    5.

3. In what ways is the work of the Spirit more powerful in the new covenant?

4. Define the following terms:

Filled with the Spirit:

Pentecost:

Two-class Christianity:

THINKING CRITICALLY

5. What do you think of the Pentecostal teaching on the baptism of the Holy Spirit as something that happens after conversion?

6. How important do you think our beliefs of the baptism of the Spirit are? What are the most significant implications of one's beliefs on this issue?

7. What is the best way to avoid allowing our experiences, or lack of experiences, to shape our beliefs more than Scripture?

PERSONAL ENGAGEMENT

8. Have you had experiences in your relationship with God that you would consider dramatic and that took you to a significantly different level of maturity in a relatively short amount of time? If not, does that ever make you feel like you are a second-class Christian? If you have, has that ever been a source of spiritual pride? How does Grudem's perspective on baptism in the Holy Spirit keep us from either of those responses?

9. Do you seek the power and presence of the Spirit as a regular part of your life as a Christian? If not, what might you be missing?

10. As you close your time in this chapter, thank God for the power and presence of the Spirit, and ask him for a growing dependence on that power and presence.

CHAPTER 40

The Perseverance of the Saints (Remaining a Christian)

OPENING PRAYER

Sovereign King, thank you that you will complete the work you have begun in those you redeem. Help me to pursue holiness as one of your saints and, along the way, to rest in your sustaining grace. In Jesus' name I pray. Amen.

CHAPTER REVIEW

1. Fill in the blanks: The perseverance of the saints means that all those who are truly _____ _____ will be kept by God's _____ and will persevere as Christians until the _____ of their _____, and that only those who _____ to the end have been truly born again.

2. Define the following terms:

Eternal security:

Assurance of salvation:

Book of Life:

Free Grace theology:

3. What are some external signs of conversion that do not necessarily demonstrate that someone is a true believer?

4. What are some indicators that someone is likely not a true believer in spite of what they say?

5. What are the primary indicators in someone's life that shows they are truly born again?

THINKING CRITICALLY

6. What verses do you find most convincing in the argument for perseverance of the saints? What verses do you find most convincing that true believers can lose their salvation? How do you reconcile these verses?

7. What are potentially negative effects of believing in the perseverance of the saints? What are potentially negative effects of believing you can lose your salvation?

8. How would you respond if someone said to you that "our assurance of salvation should be based solely on Scripture, not on our subjective evaluation of such evidence in our lives"?

PERSONAL ENGAGEMENT

9. Do you believe you can lose your salvation? If so, how has this had an impact on your life in Christ? If not, how has your belief in perseverance had an impact on your life in Christ?

10. As you consider the sources of genuine conversion that Grudem explains, would you say that they are all generally true of you?

11. As you close your time in this chapter, thank God for the finished work of Christ, and ask him to bring you greater assurance of your salvation.

CHAPTER 41

Death and the Intermediate State

OPENING PRAYER

Lord, you tell us that the wages of sin is death. Thank you that death does not have the last word; Jesus does! Help me to grieve the death in this world as the result of our rebellion against you, and give me greater and greater hope that one day the dead in Christ will rise and that our bodies and souls will no longer be tragically separated. Amen.

CHAPTER REVIEW

1. Briefly explain the main reasons that Christians die:

    1.

    2.

    3.

    4.

    5.

2. Define the following terms:

Intermediate state:

Soul sleep:

Purgatory:

Annihilationism:

THINKING CRITICALLY

3. What do you think of Grudem's argument for why we should not believe in purgatory? What are ways a belief in purgatory will affect our understanding of justification by faith?

4. Why do you think so many people believe in reincarnation? What do you think people find appealing about it?

5. What would you say to a friend who believes in reincarnation to help him or her understand the biblical view of death?

PERSONAL ENGAGEMENT

6. When Paul says that for him "to live is Christ, and to die is gain" (Phil. 1:21), can you relate to that?

7. How can a Christian view of death free us from the fear of it?

8. Do you fear death? If so, ask God to help you trust him and his powerfully effective solution to death, and ask him to give you the peace that brings.

9. To close your time in this chapter, thank God for his work in conquering death on your behalf, and ask him to continue to grow your faith in the hope of the resurrection.

CHAPTER 42

Glorification (Receiving a Resurrection Body)

OPENING PRAYER

Heavenly Father, I am grateful that you created human beings with physical bodies and said that was very good. Thank you that Jesus, too, had a physical body and that he rose bodily from the dead, and so will I! Help me to look forward to that day with great hope and live each day presenting myself, body and soul, to you as a living sacrifice. Amen.

CHAPTER REVIEW

1. Define *glorification*:

2. What does 1 Corinthians 15:12–58 teach about glorification or resurrection? Make a list of your findings.

3. Did Jewish people in the first century have any concept of resurrection? How do we know?

4. True / False: A visible brightness or radiance will surround us when we are in our resurrection bodies.

5. Fill in the blanks: When Christ _____, he will give us new _____ bodies to be like his resurrection body.

6. True / False: Inability to understand or explain something is a valid reason for rejecting the clear teaching of Scripture.

7. How is the affirmation of a resurrection related to the goodness of God's physical creation?

8. Who will be raised for judgment on the day of final judgment?

    a. Believers

    b. Unbelievers

    c. Both believers and unbelievers

    d. No one

THINKING CRITICALLY

9. What do you think the current secular culture thinks about resurrection? How could you address those beliefs based on what you have learned from this chapter, offering correction and/or hope?

PERSONAL ENGAGEMENT

10. If the resurrection were not true, how would that change your faith and your life?

11. How does the truth about bodily resurrection encourage you and provide you hope in the face of death?

12. As you close your time in this chapter, thank God for the resurrection of the dead, the future glorification of our bodies, and the hope that it provides.

CHAPTER 43

Union with Christ

OPENING PRAYER

Lord, thank you that all that is Christ's has been given to your people. His faithfulness, obedience, righteousness, and perfect sacrifice are fully ours by faith in him. Please help me to rely on the finished work of Christ on my behalf more than ever after studying this chapter. In Jesus' name I pray. Amen.

CHAPTER REVIEW

1. Fill in the blanks: _____ aspect of God's relationship to believers is in some way connected to our relationship with _____.

2. Define *union with Christ*:

3. Name and give a brief explanation of each of the four aspects of our union with Christ as outlined by Grudem.

    1.

    2.

    3.

    4.

4. When were believers chosen "in Christ"?

    a. When they believed

    b. When Jesus died

    c. Before the foundation of the world

    d. When Jesus came to earth

5. In what way were believers present throughout Christ's entire life on earth?

6. Fill in the blanks: Every stage of the _____ of redemption is given to us because we are "in _____."

7. Is being in Christ merely an individual experience? Why or why not?

8. In what area of life is imitation of Christ especially evident? Why?

9. Fill in the blanks: When we _____ like Christ we _____ like Christ.

THINKING CRITICALLY

10. If we were not in Christ, what would that mean for the idea of imputation regarding our salvation?

11. How would you respond to someone who thought it was unfair that Jesus' righteousness is considered our righteousness even though we did nothing to earn or deserve it?

PERSONAL ENGAGEMENT

12. How would it change your experience of daily life to know and truly believe that every action you do can be done "in Christ"?

13. In what ways does your life imitate Christ? Ask the Lord to help you further imitate the life of Christ.

14. To close your time in this chapter, thank God for uniting you with Christ in life, death, and resurrection.

Part 5
REVIEW QUIZ

1. Match each term with its definition:

a. Common grace
b. Election
c. Reprobation
d. Effective calling
e. Regeneration
f. Conversion
g. Saving faith

h. Repentance
i. Justification
j. Adoption
k. Sanctification
l. Perseverance of the saints
m. Glorification
n. Union with Christ

_____ An act of God the Father, speaking through the human proclamation of the gospel, in which he summons people to himself in such a way that they respond in saving faith.

_____ The grace of God by which he gives people innumerable blessings that are not part of salvation.

_____ The sovereign decision of God before creation to pass over some persons, in sorrow deciding not to save them, and to punish them for their sins, and thereby to manifest his justice.

_____ The final step in the application of redemption. It will happen when Christ returns and raises from the dead the bodies of all believers for all time who have died, and reunites them with their souls, and changes the bodies of all believers who remain alive, thereby giving all believers at the same time perfect resurrection bodies like his own.

_____ Trust in Jesus Christ as a living person for forgiveness of sins and for eternal life with God.

_____ A secret act of God in which he imparts new spiritual life to us.

_____ Our willing response to the gospel call, in which we sincerely repent of sins and place our trust in Christ for salvation.

_____ An instantaneous legal act of God in which he thinks of our sins as forgiven and Christ's righteousness as belonging to us, and declares us to be righteous in his sight.

_____ An act of God whereby he makes us members of his family.

_____ A phrase used to summarize several different relationships between believers and Christ, through which Christians receive every benefit of salvation. These relationships include the fact that we are in Christ, Christ is in us, we are like Christ, and we are with Christ.

_____ All those who are truly born again will be kept by God's power and will persevere as Christians until the end of their lives, and only those who persevere until the end have been truly born again.

_____ An act of God before creation in which he chooses some people to be saved, not on account of any foreseen merit in them, but only because of his sovereign good pleasure.

_____ A progressive work of God and believers that makes us more and more free from sin and like Christ in our actual lives.

_____ Heartfelt sorrow for sin, a renouncing of it, and a sincere commitment to forsake it and walk in obedience to Christ.

2. True / False: Being filled with the Holy Spirit always results in speaking in tongues.

3. True / False: Creation will be renewed as our bodies are renewed.

PART 6

The Doctrine of the Church

CHAPTER 44

The Church: Its Nature, Its Marks, and Its Purposes

OPENING PRAYER

Heavenly Father, thank you that you have created a people for yourself. As I learn about the church in this chapter, help me to increase my understanding, but also please help me to learn to love your bride like you do and to find my truest family among the family of God. And may we as your church be the salt and light you've created us to be. Amen.

CHAPTER REVIEW

1. Fill in the blanks: The church is the _____ of all _____ _____ for all _____.

2. True / False: *Ekklesia* is a Greek term that refers to the building that a church meets in.

3. What does Grudem mean when he says that the church is both visible and invisible?

4. What are the similarities and differences between the church and Israel?

5. What are the similarities and differences between the church and the kingdom of God?

6. The Reformation understanding of the marks of the true church are:

    a. Missions and evangelism

    b. Building and budget

    c. Word and sacrament

    d. Mission and vision

THINKING CRITICALLY

7. What are metaphors for the church that the Bible uses that are especially helpful in the society in which you live?

8. What are metaphors for the church that the Bible uses that are particularly difficult to understand in the society in which you live? How would you explain them to someone so they can understand them better?

9. What do you think of Grudem's explanation of the relationship between the church and Israel? Have you understood and used those terms as basically the same thing before reading this chapter? Will you use them any differently now?

PERSONAL ENGAGEMENT

10. The church is the bride of Christ, and he bought the church with his blood. Does your love for the church reflect the love God has for the church? Why or why not?

11. If you are a Christian, are you meaningfully committed to a local church? If so, how has this been of benefit to you? If not, what have you been missing out on according to what you read in this chapter?

12. Is there one metaphor that the Bible uses for the church that is especially helpful to you? What is it about that one that makes it so?

13. As you close out this chapter, spend some time in worship of God for the gift of the church.

CHAPTER 45

The Purity and Unity of the Church

OPENING PRAYER

Lord, you are the husband of your people, and you have promised that we will be pure and perfectly unified like you are one day. As I continue to learn about what it means to be a part of your church, help me to love her and seek after her growth in holiness and oneness. Amen.

CHAPTER REVIEW

1. Fill in the blanks: The purity of the church is its _____ of _____ from wrong _____ and _____, and its degree of _____ to God's _____ will for the church.

2. Fill in the blanks: The unity of the church is its _____ of _____ from _____ among true Christians.

3. Briefly explain good and bad reasons for separation in the church.

4. Define the following terms:

Eastern church:

Western church:

Separation:

THINKING CRITICALLY

5. Grudem says that liberal Protestantism is humanistic and primarily man-centered rather than God-centered. Do you agree with that assessment? If so, in what ways you have seen conservative Protestantism exhibit those same characteristics?

6. Can you provide an example of a time in the church when you saw a serious pursuit of purity without it being unnecessarily divisive?

7. Do you think the differences between the Protestant and Roman Catholic traditions that Grudem cites are significant enough to cause a separation? Why or why not?

PERSONAL ENGAGEMENT

8. If you regularly attend a church, as you look over the list of the twelve factors that make a church pure, on a scale of 0 (not at all) to 10 (outstanding), how would you evaluate your church with respect to each factor?

9. If you are a Christian, do you think you can say that you are living in a way that is striving to build up the church (1 Cor. 14:12) and seeking its purity and unity? Why or why not?

10. As you finish this chapter, pray that God will use you as an influence for purity and unity in your church.

CHAPTER 46

The Power of the Church

OPENING PRAYER

Lord, thank you that you have promised that the gates of hell will not prevail against your church and that you will accomplish the work you have begun in us. Even though we often look frail, sinful, and broken, please give me great hope and confidence in the bright future and present work you are doing in and through your people. In Jesus' name I pray. Amen.

CHAPTER REVIEW

1. Fill in the blanks: The power of the church is its _____ _____ to carry on spiritual _____, _____ the gospel, and exercise _____ _____.

2. Define the following terms:

Keys of the kingdom:

Excommunication:

Binding and loosing:

Take up the sword:

3. How do the power of the church and the power of the state differ?

4. What are the three primary reasons for church discipline?

    1.

    2.

    3.

5. How should the discipline of church leaders differ from those who are members of a church but not leaders?

THINKING CRITICALLY

6. It seems that many churches today do not practice church discipline in a consistently biblical way. Why do you think that may be the case?

7. The Bible clearly commands Christians to submit to governing authorities and their church authorities. Why do you think the word *submission* has such negative connotations for many people? How should a Christian think so that he or she learns to love the idea and practice of biblical submission?

PERSONAL ENGAGEMENT

8. Have you ever seen church discipline practiced in a way that was edifying and God honoring? If so, what were the key factors that contributed to making it so?

9. Would you say that you regularly and joyfully submit to the authority of the church? If so, what does that look like, and if not, what is preventing you from doing so?

10. As you complete this chapter, pray that you would understand better why God gave us human authorities, and ask that he would increase your ability to humbly submit to the authorities he has put in your life.

CHAPTER 47

Church Government

OPENING PRAYER

Lord, thank you that you are a God of order and that you have given order to your church. Help me to joyfully submit to the shepherds in my local church, because they will have to answer to you one day for how they cared for your flock. Amen.

CHAPTER REVIEW

1. How does church government differ from doctrines like the Trinity and substitutionary atonement?

2. Define *church officer*. What other often-used terms are included in this broad category according to Grudem?

3. Fill in the blanks: Many other people exercise _____ in the church, but we do not say they have an "_____" because they do not need formal public recognition for their gifts to _____.

4. What are the two uses of the word *apostle* in Scripture?

5. Circle the qualifications for being an apostle:

Eyewitness of the resurrection

Expert in the law

Educated

Commissioned by Christ

Feeling equipped

6. True / False: Only the twelve disciples of Jesus were apostles.

7. Fill in the blanks: In place of _____ apostles present in the church to teach and govern it, we have instead the _____ of the apostles in the books of the _____ _____.

8. What is the consistent pattern of the main governing group in New Testament churches?

   a. A head pastor

   b. Plural elders

   c. Gifted teachers

   d. An apostle

9. What other names are used for elders in the New Testament?

10. Explain Grudem's stance on the phrase "husband of one wife."

11. What responsibilities might the role of deacon have included in the early church?

12. Why might it be important or helpful to include the whole church in the selection of leaders?

13. Briefly describe each major system of church government:

Episcopalian:

Presbyterian:

Congregational:

    Single elder/pastor:

    Plural local elders:

    Corporate board:

Pure democracy:

No government but the Holy Spirit:

14. True / False: The Bible teaches that women are never to teach the Bible. Explain.

THINKING CRITICALLY

15. How would you respond to someone who claimed that no sort of office is needed in a church setting?

16. If someone came to you claiming to be an apostle, how could you respond graciously and biblically to that claim?

17. Compare and contrast the egalitarian and complementarian views on women in church offices. Which arguments do you find most persuasive on either side?

PERSONAL ENGAGEMENT

18. Before reading this chapter, had you thought much about the biblical model of church leadership? Based on your reading of this chapter, has your opinion on the subject changed?

19. How can you more faithfully engage in your church with a greater understanding of the authority in church leadership established by God?

20. To close your time in this chapter, thank God for his establishment of leadership in the church, from the apostles until now, and ask him to continue to raise up faithful leaders and help you to submit to them.

CHAPTER 48

Means of Grace within the Church

OPENING PRAYER

Lord, thank you that you have given us ways that we are able to draw near to you and become like Christ. I pray that I would faithfully avail myself to these means of grace and bear fruit of the Spirit as he works through them. Amen.

CHAPTER REVIEW

1. Fill in the blanks: All of the _____ we experience in this life are ultimately _____— they are all of _____.

2. Define *means of grace*:

3. What is the difference between the Catholic view of the "sacraments" and the Protestant view of the "means of grace"?

4. How does the teaching of God's Word provide blessing to the believer's life?

5. A measure of blessing should be expected connected to baptism because:

    a. The water sanctifies the believer.

    b. Jesus commanded his church to baptize.

    c. It is a public event.

6. Fill in the blanks: The Lord's Supper is not simply an _____ meal among human beings—it is a _____ with Christ, in his presence and at his table.

7. True / False: You can participate in the Lord's Supper wrongly.

8. With the increase of genuine fellowship in a church comes an increase of:

    a. Sanctification

    b. Sin

    c. Prayer

    d. The Lord's Supper

9. Fill in the blanks: When we enter that _____ realm of activity and _____ to the Lord in worship, God also _____ to us.

10. Why is worship one of the primary means of grace available to the church?

11. How are the spiritual gifts a means of grace?

12. What does an emphasis on the fellowship of believers help to overcome?

13. Name a few forms of ministry that Christians can use to bless an individual in the church.

14. Where do all of the means of grace occur?

    a. Within homes

    b. In the world

    c. In the church

THINKING CRITICALLY

15. What might be an argument for the practice of footwashing in the church as a means of grace?

16. Pick one of the major distinctions between Protestants and Catholics in the "Additional Note" in chapter 45, and respond to it with a paragraph explaining a biblical view on the subject.

PERSONAL ENGAGEMENT

17. Which means of grace does your church practice regularly? How do you engage in these practices yourself?

18. How have you found the means of grace to be a blessing to your life?

19. To close your time in this chapter, thank God for the various means of grace that he has given the church, and ask him to help you engage further in them for his glory and the good of the church.

CHAPTER 49

Baptism

OPENING PRAYER

Lord, thank you that by faith I have union with Christ and that I have died and been raised with him. Enable me to walk more fully in the complete identification with Christ that is displayed in my baptism. Please empower me to leave behind life in the flesh and to walk in the newness of life I have in Christ. In Jesus' name I pray. Amen.

CHAPTER REVIEW

1. Why do some Protestants prefer the word *ordinance* over *sacrament*?

2. Define the Baptistic position put forth by Grudem. What is another common name for this position?

3. The mode of baptism in Scripture is:

    a. Sprinkling

    b. Watering

    c. Immersion

4. What is the relationship between the union with Christ in his death and baptism by immersion?

5. Fill in the blanks: Baptism is a _____ of beginning the Christian _____.

6. What do you think is the strongest evidence that baptism is for those who have received the gospel and trusted in Christ?

7. Explain the covenant argument for paedobaptism.

8. What are the three means of entrance into the church?

   1.

   2.

   3.

9. Why can paedobaptists affirm neither the Roman Catholic view of baptism nor the Baptist view of baptism?

10. True / False: Baptism is necessary for salvation.

THINKING CRITICALLY

11. What effect do you think the mode of baptism persons experience might have on the way they think about and experience their lives as followers of Jesus?

12. What are possible misunderstandings of the Christian life that could be the result of believing in infant baptism?

13. What are possible misunderstandings of the Christian life that could result from a belief in believer's baptism?

14. How would you respond to someone who believes a person must be baptized to be saved?

PERSONAL ENGAGEMENT

15. How significant has your baptism been in your life as a Christian? Has it served as a marker or memory that has encouraged your faith? If not, why do you think that is?

16. How significant do you think baptism is? If you had a friend who is a Christian but had not been baptized and did not plan to be, how would you counsel him or her?

17. Close your time in this chapter by thanking God for your union with Christ by faith, which your baptism points to.

CHAPTER 50

The Lord's Supper

OPENING PRAYER

Dear Lord, I am profoundly grateful that Jesus took my punishment and died in my place. Thank you for the privilege of remembering this along with your people in the Lord's Supper. Every time I take it, please enable me to do it with the correct contrition and joy. And please help me to value the body of Christ more as we remember the body and blood together. Amen.

CHAPTER REVIEW

1. What are the two ordinances/sacraments that were instituted by Jesus for the church to observe?

1.

2.

2. How is the Lord's Supper symbolic of Jesus' death?

3. When Christians participate in the Lord's Supper, they (circle all that apply):

a. Give a clear sign of unity

b. Remember that Jesus died for them

c. Are saved

d. Participate in the benefits of Jesus' death

e. Receive spiritual nourishment

4. How is the Lord's Supper related to the blessings of salvation?

5. Fill in the blank: When I take the Lord's Supper, I _____ my faith in Christ.

6. Define the following terms:

Ex opere operato:

Transubstantiation:

7. True / False: The Roman Catholic view of the Lord's Supper (or Mass) is that there is a continuation of Christ's sacrifice for our sins each time the Mass is celebrated.

8. Explain the Lutheran view of the Lord's Supper:

9. Explain the symbolic or spiritual presence view of the Lord's Supper:

10. Who should participate in the Lord's Supper?

    a. Only men

    b. Only those who believe

    c. Anyone who comes to church

    d. Anyone can participate in the Lord's Supper.

11. Fill in the blanks: Baptism is clearly a symbol of _____ the Christian life, while the Lord's Supper is clearly a symbol of _____ the Christian life.

12. What are the qualifications for taking the Lord's Supper?

    1.

    2.

    3.

13. Who, according to Grudem, would be excluded from administering the Lord's Supper?

    a. Church leaders

    b. Men

    c. Women

    d. Unbelievers

THINKING CRITICALLY

14. Compare and contrast transubstantiation, the Lutheran view, and the symbolic view of the Lord's Supper. What are the strengths and weaknesses of each view?

PERSONAL ENGAGEMENT

15. In what ways have your views on the Lord's Supper changed as a result of reading this chapter?

16. How could you change your engagement with the Lord's Supper to make it a richer experience? Consider especially section B on the meaning of the Lord's Supper.

17. To end your time in this chapter, thank Jesus for the gift of his sacrifice on the cross, and ask him to help you further love him and rightly participate in the Lord's Supper, in thankfulness and unity with other believers.

CHAPTER 51

Worship

OPENING PRAYER

Heavenly Father, offering you praise is an awesome privilege. Apart from the Spirit's work there would be nothing Godward in us. All we should hear from you is "Depart from me," but because of Jesus, we are able to boldly approach your throne. You are indeed worthy! Amen.

CHAPTER REVIEW

1. What is Grudem addressing when he speaks of worship in this chapter?

    a. Anything done to the glory of God

    b. The music and words that Christians direct to God in praise

    c. All of the Christian life

2. Fill in the blanks: Worship is the _____ of _____ _____ in his presence with our _____ and _____.

3. What does reflecting on the purpose of worship remind us of?

4. Why should our worship services be oriented toward calling attention to God and causing people to think about him?

5. Fill in the blanks: We probably experience _____ in God more fully in _____ than in any other activity in this life.

6. Why can continual praise not last forever in this age?

7. What does God do when we worship him?

  a. Scoff

  b. Take delight in it

  c. Smile

  d. He is unmoved

8. How is new covenant worship distinct from old covenant worship?

9. Of what benefit is worship to us?

10. How is worship related to spiritual warfare?

11. Fill in the blank: Worship is doing the _____ of God.

12. What is meant by the phrase "in spirit and truth" from John 4:23?

  a. Not worshiping by raising your hands or dancing

  b. Worshiping in the spiritual realm

  c. Remaining emotionless in worship

  d. Only worshiping with traditional hymns

13. True / False: Genuine worship can be self-generated or worked up within ourselves.

14. What are some of the ways that we can make worship more effective?

15. Is the setting of worship important? Why or why not?

16. Why does Grudem advocate for singing hymns in church?

THINKING CRITICALLY

17. How might worship be a means of evangelism? Would it be right for churches to orient their worship services in light of this? Why or why not?

18. Contrast the "look at me" and "look at God" approaches to worship in church.

PERSONAL ENGAGEMENT

19. When you worship, do you feel as if you are worshiping "in spirit and truth"? Why or why not?

20. How could you help in making your worship experience in church, as well as the experience of others, better or more fulfilling?

21. As you end your time in this chapter, spend time in worship to the Lord. Pick one of the songs mentioned in *Systematic Theology*, and sing it out loud. Thank the Lord for providing us means to worship and for being a God worthy of worship.

CHAPTER 52

Gifts of the Holy Spirit: (1) General Questions

OPENING PRAYER

Lord, thank you for the sovereign grace of the Holy Spirit as he distributes his gifts to the church. I pray that I would seek the gifts of the Spirit for the good of the body of Christ and for your glory, not for my own exaltation. Amen.

CHAPTER REVIEW

1. Define *spiritual gift*:

2. True / False: There was less powerful activity of the Holy Spirit in the lives of most believers in the Old Testament.

3. Fill in the blanks: When Jesus began his ministry, he came bringing the _____ and _____ of the Holy Spirit in his _____.

4. When did the pouring out of the Holy Spirit occur?

    a. The Feast of Tabernacles

    b. Pentecost

    c. Passover

    d. Easter

5. True / False: The early church was a miracle-working church.

6. What is the purpose of spiritual gifts?

7. How do spiritual gifts give a foretaste of the age to come?

8. How many spiritual gifts are there?

   a. Two

   b. Twenty

   c. Three

   d. An unknown amount

9. True / False: A spiritual gift will always express itself the same way no matter who has it.

10. Fill in the blanks: God gives the church an amazing _____ of spiritual gifts, and they are all tokens of his varied _____.

11. How is it that spiritual gifts vary in strength?

12. How long do Christians have spiritual gifts? Explain your answer.

13. How does the definition of the word *miracle* affect the discussion of spiritual gifts?

14. True / False: The Bible distinguishes between miraculous and nonmiraculous gifts.

15. How can people discern what their spiritual gifts are? (Circle all that apply.)

    a. Ask what gifts are needed for building up the church.

    b. Do self-examination.

    c. Ask God for wisdom.

    d. Try ministering in various places.

16. Fill in the blanks: The _____ gifts are those that _____ up the church more and bring more _____ to others.

17. Spiritual gifts are given to:

    a. Mature believers

    b. Believers active in ministry

    c. All believers

18. True / False: We should evaluate spiritual maturity based on spiritual gifts.

19. Describe the beliefs of the following three groups regarding spiritual gifts:

Cessationist:

Continuationist:

"Open but cautious":

20. When does Grudem say that the partial gifts will pass away?

21. True / False: Many continuationists (or noncessationists) claim that prophecy today is equal to Scripture.

22. Does the abuse of a gift mean that we must prohibit the proper use of a gift? Explain your answer.

THINKING CRITICALLY

23. How would you respond to those who say they cannot engage in an activity because that is not their spiritual gift (e.g., serving, evangelism, faith)?

24. Do you agree with Grudem when he says that the continuation of prophecy does not challenge the sufficiency of Scripture? Why or why not?

25. What could cessationist churches learn from charismatics? What could charismatics learn from cessationists?

PERSONAL ENGAGEMENT

26. What spiritual gifts have you seen most clearly at work in and through your life? How do you know they are gifts of the Spirit and not just things you're naturally good at?

27. Have you ever experienced any of the miraculous gifts of the Spirit? Which ones? Did you see them have a clearly edifying impact on others for the glory of God?

28. As you close your time in this chapter, thank God for *all* his gifts, and ask him to increase your dependence on the Spirit.

CHAPTER 53

Gifts of the Holy Spirit: (2) Specific Questions

OPENING PRAYER

Almighty God, I thank you for your miraculous power, and I'm grateful that you are still powerfully at work in and through the church. Give us discernment and wisdom to "test the spirits" and to know if they are from you or not. I pray that we, your people, would be eager to see you work and eager for your kingdom to be advancing greatly in our day. Amen.

CHAPTER REVIEW

1. Define *prophecy*:

2. What other meaning did the word *prophet* have at the time of the New Testament?

3. True / False: Grudem concludes that prophecies in the church today should be considered human words, not God's words, and not equal to God's words in authority.

4. How does Thomas Schreiner distinguish between prophecy and impressions?

5. Explain Grudem's definition of the word *revelation* as used by Paul.

6. How can prophecy be a sign for nonbelievers?

7. Fill in the blanks: God communicates _____ and _____ with his _____ throughout _____ _____.

8. Define *teaching*:

9. Compare and contrast prophesying and teaching.

10. When will Christians experience the full possession of redemption from physical illness?

   a. Anytime they pray

   b. When they become Christians

   c. At the coming of Christ

11. What ought to be the relationship between praying for healing and the use of medicine?

12. What three mistakes can be made in regard to praying for healing?

    1.

    2.

    3.

13. What is the pastoral solution to these mistakes that Grudem suggests?

14. Fill in the blanks: In everything God should receive _____, and our joy and _____ in him should increase.

15. What word does Grudem advocate "tongue" should be translated as?

    a. Angelic

    b. Miraculous

    c. Language

    d. Voice

16. True / False: The phenomenon of speaking in tongues is not unique to the new covenant age.

17. Define *speaking in tongues*:

18. True / False: Speaking in tongues as described in Scripture is "ecstatic speech."

19. Match the activity with the right context by drawing a line between the two:

Tongues with interpretation   Alone

Tongues without interpretation   In the church

20. Define *the gift of interpretation*:

21. True / False: All have the gift of speaking in tongues.

22. Define *distinguishing between spirits*:

THINKING CRITICALLY

23. What do you think of Grudem's view of the ongoing nature of prophecy in the New Testament era, as distinct from prophecy in the Old Testament? Do you think he sufficiently distinguishes between the authority of Old Testament prophets and those expressing prophetic words in the new covenant? Why or why not?

24. Do you think Grudem sufficiently distinguishes between the authority of Scripture and the authority of prophecy today? What do you think of people using the term "God spoke to me" in reference to getting a "word from the Lord"?

PERSONAL ENGAGEMENT

25. How much do you seek the leading and direction of the Spirit in your life? What would need to change for you to be more Spirit led in your life?

26. Do you resonate with those who are more objective in their faith or those who are more subjective in their faith? How could you, as Grudem advises, allow the other perspective to influence you in a way that increases your own personal relationship with God?

27. To close your time in this chapter, thank God for giving spiritual gifts, and ask him to give you discernment to rightly interpret the Word of God and the work of God in the world today.

1. True / False: The church is invisible and visible, local, and universal.

2. The church has power in all but which of the following areas?

    a. Spiritual warfare

    b. Enacting state decisions

    c. Proclaiming the gospel

    d. Exercising church discipline

3. True / False: The purpose of church discipline is to show the power of the church.

4. True / False: Anyone can be a church officer.

5. Means of grace occur:

    a. Primarily in the context of one-on-one discipleship

    b. Only directly from God to one believer

    c. In the fellowship of the church

6. True / False: Paedobaptists argue that infants should not be baptized.

7. Transubstantiation argues that:

    a. The bread and wine symbolize Christ's body and blood.

    b. The bread and wine become Christ's body and blood.

    c. Christ's body and blood are in, with, and under the bread and wine.

8. True/ False: The purpose of worship is glorifying God.

9. Match the gift of the Spirit with its definition:

a. Prophecy   d. Healing
b. Teaching   e. Tongues
c. Miracles   f. Words of wisdom/knowledge

_____ The ability to explain Scripture and apply it to people's lives.

_____ When God's power is manifested in an evident way to further God's purposes in a situation.

_____ God granting a partial foretaste of the perfect health that will be ours for eternity.

_____ Prayer or praise spoken in syllables not understood by the speaker.

_____ The ability to speak with wisdom or with knowledge in various situations.

_____ Telling something that God has spontaneously brought to mind.

PART 7

The Doctrine of the Future

CHAPTER 54

The Return of Christ: When and How?

OPENING PRAYER

Lord, thank you for the blessed hope of Christ's return. Please enable me to live my whole life in light of his second coming. Fill my soul with hope and longing to see him when the dead in Christ shall rise with him. *Maranatha!* Amen.

CHAPTER REVIEW

1. Define the following terms:

Eschatology:

Personal eschatology:

General eschatology:

The preterist view:

Imminent:

Maranatha:

Parousia:

2. Fill in the blanks: The return of Christ will be _____, _____, visible, and _____.

3. What are the six signs that the Bible says must happen before Christ returns?

    1.

    2.

    3.

    4.

    5.

    6.

THINKING CRITICALLY

4. What is the importance of the return of Christ being bodily, not just spiritual? What would be the implications of a merely spiritual return, especially for the way we view our resurrected state and the way we view our bodies now?

5. How do you navigate the tension between the biblical teaching of being ready and eagerly awaiting for and seeking to discern the times and at the same time resting in God's sovereignty because no one knows the time of his return?

6. In your opinion, what are the most important and clear teachings in the Bible about the second coming? What are the issues that Christians should allow for diversity of perspectives?

PERSONAL ENGAGEMENT

7. Do you long for Jesus to return? If so, what in your experiences and thinking have led to that longing? If not, what do you think may be missing from your perspective?

8. How do you think suffering and persecution play into a growing longing for the return of Christ?

9. What are ways we should practically "be ready" for Christ's return? In what ways are you storing up treasures rather than on earth?

10. As you close this chapter, praise and thank God that one day Jesus will return, and ask him to give you a greater longing for that day.

CHAPTER 55

The Millennium

OPENING PRAYER

King of Kings, I thank you that the day is coming when your will will forever be done on earth as it is in heaven. This is your world—you made it and are remaking and redeeming it. I look forward to the day when Jesus will reign once and for all, vanquish the powers of darkness, and put an end to sin and death. Amen.

CHAPTER REVIEW

1. Define the following terms:

Millennium:

Amillennialism:

Postmillennialism:

Classic/historic premillennialism:

Pretribulational/dispensational premillennialism:

Tribulation:

Rapture:

2. True/False: The amillennial view teaches that Jesus will not return until after the secret rapture of God's people.

3. True/False: The postmillennial view can easily lead to passivity and not seeking to see God work powerfully even before Jesus returns.

4. Which of the following is the view that Jesus will secretly return for his people before he sets foot on earth:

    a. Millennium view

    b. Rapture

    c. Postmillennial view

    d. *Eschaton*

    e. Preterist view

THINKING CRITICALLY

5. Among the issues discussed in this chapter, which ones do you think are clear and important enough to add to a statement of belief for a church, and which ones should be considered "disputable matters"? How do you decide which is which?

6. The various views of the millennium discussed in this book come to different conclusions as they try to synthesize the relevant texts. Which one do you think does the best job and why?

7. How we understand certain texts sets a precedent for how we approach other ones as well. Do you think there are ways of interpreting texts in any of the views that you would not want to be used elsewhere in the Bible?

PERSONAL ENGAGEMENT

8. What do you think about the possibility of God's children going through the great tribulation? Do you think God would allow this? Why or why not?

9. Which view of the millennium do you agree with? How does this view affect the way you view your life today?

10. Do you long for the kingdom of God to be established on earth? Why? Do you pray for that and seek to bring about realities of the kingdom even before it arrives fully? In what ways?

11. Close your time in this chapter by praying that God's will would be done on earth as it is in heaven.

CHAPTER 56

The Final Judgment and Eternal Punishment

OPENING PRAYER

Judge of the earth, I am grateful that your perfect justice will one day be poured out, and all the wrongs of human history will be made right. Thank you that Jesus was judged in my place so I do not need to fear that day. Please give me boldness in warning people to flee the wrath to come and find freedom from eternal punishment in Christ. Amen.

CHAPTER REVIEW

1. Define the following terms:

Conditional immortality:

Universalism:

Great white throne judgment:

Eternal conscious punishment:

Annihilationism:

2. True / False: Unbelievers, believers, and angels will all face a final judgment.

3. What is the purpose of the final judgment of believers?

4. Briefly summarize the four moral applications Grudem gives for the final judgment:

   1.

   2.

   3.

   4.

5. Fill in the blanks: Hell is a place of _____ conscious _____ for the _____.

THINKING CRITICALLY

6. What do you think of the idea of degrees of rewards in heaven? How will all believers be able to enjoy heaven equally when some believers will receive greater degrees of rewards?

7. If hell did not exist, what effect would that have on the character of God? What would it be like to live in a world where God was not eventually going to bring perfect justice to all the wrongs that have ever been committed?

8. Several passages speak of the saints offering praise and gratitude for the judgment and punishment of the wicked that God will finally bring (e.g., Rev. 19:3). How could hell and punishment be something we could be grateful for?

PERSONAL ENGAGEMENT

9. As a Christian, when you consider that you will be part of judging the world, how does that have an impact on your understanding of your union with Christ now?

10. Do you often think about Jesus as the coming judge of the world? How should thinking of Jesus as the judge of all the earth increase your trust in and healthy fear of him?

11. As you complete your study of this chapter, thank God that you will not have to fear the day that Jesus returns and holds the whole world accountable but can look forward to it with great hope because of the finished work of Christ on your behalf.

CHAPTER 57

The New Heavens and New Earth

OPENING PRAYER

Lord, I long for the day when sin will be no more and you will wipe away every tear and defeat sin and Satan and bring your work in redemptive history to a glorious consummation. Help me live every day looking forward to that great day when your people from every tongue and tribe and nation gather around your throne praising your name forever. In the name of the Father, Son, and Holy Spirit I pray Amen.

CHAPTER REVIEW

1. True / False: The Bible teaches us that there will be new heavens and a new earth—an entirely renewed creation—and we will live there with God.

2. Define *heaven*:

3. Fill in the blanks: Heaven is a _____, not just a _____ of _____.

4. What is some of the biblical evidence that heaven is a place?

5. Fill in the blanks: The _____ creation will be _____ and we will continue to _____ and _____ in it.

6. In the new heavens and the new earth, we will:

    a. Live in a disembodied state

    b. Live in resurrected bodies

    c. Live a life totally unlike our own

7. Fill in the blanks: The new creation will not be "_____" but will include an _____ succession of _____.

8. What does the doctrine of the new creation provide motivation for?

9. Fill in the blanks: The new creation will be a _____ of great _____ and _____ and _____ in the presence of _____.

10. In the heavenly city we will be _____ the power and holiness of the presence of God's glory. (Put the correct letter in the blank.)

    a. Put to death

    b. Able to endure

    c. Unable to see

11. True / False: When we finally see the Lord face-to-face, our hearts will want nothing else.

THINKING CRITICALLY

12. Grudem says that heaven will be a place and not just a state of mind. Do you think most Christians have an overly spiritualized idea of heaven that is not sufficiently physical and located in a place? If so, what implications would this have for how we view the physical and places now?

13. If, as Grudem says, God and humans will experience a succession of moments in heaven, how can we reconcile that with common conceptions of eternity?

PERSONAL ENGAGEMENT

14. How does the teaching that we will eat in our resurrected eternal state shape the way you view food this side of eternity?

15. Does the idea that we will work, play, eat, create, and enjoy life in many ways that are similar to how we experience life now increase your desire for heaven?

16. As you close your time in this chapter, thank God for the future reality of the new heavens and new earth, and pray, "Come, Lord Jesus!" (Rev. 22:20)

1. What is the study of future events often called?

  a. Future study

  b. Eschatology

  c. Endology

2. True / False: There will be a sudden, personal, visible, bodily return of Christ.

3. Who knows when Christ will return?

  a. Jesus

  b. The Spirit

  c. The Father

  d. All believers

4. Match the following statements with the corresponding belief about the millennium:

  a. Amillennialism

  b. Postmillennialism

  c. Premillennialism

  _____ There will be no future millennium.
  _____ Believers will reign with Christ on earth.
  _____ Christ will return after the millennium.
  _____ The present church age will continue until Christ's return.
  _____ Christ will come back before the millennium.
  _____ A "millennial age" of peace and righteousness on earth will occur before Christ's return.
  _____ All of the end-time events will happen immediately after Christ's return.
  _____ After the tribulation at the end of the church age, Christ will return to establish a millennial kingdom.
  _____ Optimism about the power of the gospel to bring about much good in the world.

5. True / False: There will be a great final judgment of believers and unbelievers.

6. Who will participate in the judging at the final judgment?

    a. Jesus

    b. Angels

    c. Believers

    d. Demons

7. True / False: Physical creation will be renewed at the time of the final judgment, including our physical bodies.

Appendix: God's Attributes

The study of God's attributes is worth spending time on. We highly suggest memorizing the definitions of each attribute so that you are better equipped to worship God well and to describe his character to others.

1. Independence: God does not need us or the rest of creation for anything, yet we and the rest of creation can glorify him and bring him joy.
2. Unchangeableness/Immutability: God is unchanging in his being, perfections, purposes, and promises, yet God does act and feel emotions, and he acts and feels differently in response to different situations.
3. Eternity: God has no beginning, end, or succession of moments in his own being, and he sees all time equally vividly, yet God sees events and acts in time.
4. Omnipresence: God does not have size or spatial dimensions and is present at every point of space with his whole being, yet God acts differently in different places.
5. Unity: God is not divided into parts, yet we see different attributes of God emphasized at different times.
6. Spirituality: God exists as a being who is not made of any matter, has no parts or dimensions, is unable to be perceived by our bodily senses, and is more excellent than any other kind of existence.
7. Invisibility: God's total essence, all of his spiritual being, will never be able to be seen by us, yet God still shows himself to us partially in this age and more fully in the age to come.
8. Knowledge (Omniscience): God fully knows himself and all things actual and possible in one simple and eternal act.
9. Wisdom: God always chooses the best goals and the best means to those goals.
10. Truthfulness/Faithfulness: God is the true God, and all his knowledge and words are both true and the final standard of truth.
11. Goodness: God is the final standard of good, and all God is and does is worthy of approval.
12. Love: God eternally gives of himself to others.
13. Mercy: God demonstrates goodness toward those in misery and distress.
14. Grace: God demonstrates goodness toward those who deserve only punishment.
15. Patience: God demonstrates goodness in the withholding of punishment toward those who sin over a period of time.
16. Holiness: God is separated from sin and devoted to seeking his own honor.
17. Peace/Order: In God's being and in his actions, he is separate from all confusion and disorder, yet he is continually active in innumerable well-ordered, fully controlled, simultaneous actions.
18. Righteousness/Justice: God always acts in accordance with what is right and is himself the final standard of what is right.
19. Jealousy: God continually seeks to protect his own honor.

20. Wrath: God intensely hates all sin.
21. Will: God approves and determines to bring about every action necessary for the existence and activity of himself and all creation.
22. Freedom: God does whatever he pleases.
23. Omnipotence (Power/Sovereignty): God is able to do all his holy will.
24. Perfection: God completely possesses all excellent qualities and lacks no part of any qualities that would be desirable for him.
25. Blessedness: God delights fully in himself and in all that reflects his character.
26. Beauty: God is the sum of all desirable qualities.
27. Glory: Created brightness surrounds God's revelation of himself.